INTRODUCING
Aristotle

Rupert Woodfin and Judy Groves

Edited by Richard Appignanesi

ICON BOOKS UK   TOTEM BOOKS USA

Published in the United Kingdom
in 2001 by Icon Books Ltd.,
Grange Road, Duxford,
Cambridge CB2 4QF
e-mail: info@iconbooks.co.uk
www.iconbooks.co.uk

Sold in the UK, Europe, South Africa
and Asia by Faber and Faber Ltd.,
3 Queen Square, London WC1N 3AU
or their agents

Distributed in the UK, Europe,
South Africa and Asia by
Macmillan Distribution Ltd.,
Houndmills, Basingstoke RG21 6XS

Published in Australia
in 2001 by Allen & Unwin Pty. Ltd.,
PO Box 8500, 83 Alexander Street,
Crows Nest, NSW 2065

Reprinted 2002

Published in the United States
in 2001 by Totem Books
Inquiries to: Icon Books Ltd.,
Grange Road, Duxford,
Cambridge CB2 4QF, UK
e-mail: info@iconbooks.co.uk
www.iconbooks.co.uk

In the United States,
distributed to the trade by
National Book Network Inc.,
4720 Boston Way, Lanham,
Maryland 20706

Distributed in Canada by
Penguin Books Canada,
10 Alcorn Avenue, Suite 300,
Toronto, Ontario M4V 3B2

ISBN 1 84046 233 7

Originating editor: Richard Appignanesi

Printed and bound in Australia
by McPherson's Printing Group, Victoria

A Universal Mind

The Master of those who know.
Dante Alighieri (1265-1321), poet of *The Divine Comedy*

Aristotle has been described as the most intelligent person who ever lived. He had an impact on human culture, understanding and knowledge that is difficult to match. Many of the ways in which we think can be traced back to him and his work, all too often unacknowledged today. In particular, the rational, scientific and technological culture that pervades much of the Western world owes more to him than to anyone else. He also made major contributions to the development of ethics, psychology, biology, politics and our appreciation of literature.

Aristotle's Family Background

From a distance of two and a half thousand years, Aristotle remains a shadowy figure.

It may be that the family had acted in this role for some generations of Macedonian Kings. The medical background is also significant. Medicine, even then, would have depended on acute observation, and this characterizes all of Aristotle's work.

It is not known whether Aristotle practised medicine during his lifetime, but he did say later, rather pompously …

A MAN IS ADEQUATELY EDUCATED IF HE KNOWS THE THEORY OF MEDICINE BUT DOES NOT HAVE THE PRACTICAL EXPERIENCE.

He probably had a prosperous childhood, in a comfortable rather than magnificent court, where a high priority was put on combining theoretical wisdom with pragmatic action.

Education in Athens

Aristotle lost both his parents while still a youth and passed into the care of Proxenus, who was probably a relative of his father. His intelligence must have been evident, because at seventeen he was sent to complete his education in Athens. The Thracian scholars must have become exasperated with a brilliant pupil for whom they could do nothing more. Shortly after he arrived in Athens, he joined Plato's Academy.

PLATO (c. 428-347 BC) WAS ALREADY FAMOUS FOR HIS OWN PHILOSOPHICAL IDEAS AND HIS ACCOUNTS OF SOCRATES (470-399 BC).

Plato's reputation attracted students and scholars from all over the eastern Mediterranean, as well as the sons of prosperous and powerful Athenians.

The Symposium

Plato encouraged penetrating discussions of obscure and difficult topics, but also taught the youth of Athens as a preparation for their adult life.

PARTICIPATION IN CIVIC AFFAIRS IS A DUTY FOR CITIZENS OF ATHENS.

SOME TRAINING IN POLITICS AND ETHICS IS NEEDED.

*DINNERS IN ATHENS, WHERE STUDENTS AND OTHERS DISCUSS PHILOSOPHICAL ISSUES, ARE CALLED **SYMPOSIA.***

PLATO

A symposium could be sublimely intellectual or downright orgiastic. We should not, however, be thinking about the Academy in terms of examinations or qualifications. It sounds like the ideal life, and Aristotle's later writings seem to indicate that he thought so.

Aristotle and Plato

Aristotle stayed for about twenty years in Plato's Academy and must have become a very senior member. We know frustratingly little about the relationship between the two most significant philosophers in the greatest philosophical period of Western history. The intellectual legacies of Plato and Aristotle are sharply divergent, but this divergence may have taken place after Aristotle left the Academy. On the other hand, he may have, with the arrogance of youth, opposed Plato's ideas from the start.

PLATO CALLED HIM "THE INTELLIGENCE OF THE SCHOOL".

I ALSO SAID THAT ARISTOTLE NEEDED "A BRIDLE RATHER THAN A SPUR".

AND I REFERRED TO PLATO'S ACADEMY AS "OUR FRIENDS".

So it is safe to assume that the relationship might have been acrimonious from time to time, but was not bitter. **Isocrates** (436-338 BC) had a rival school to the Academy. Aristotle wrote and spoke on the opposing Academy "team".

Murky Affairs

Plato died in 347 BC and Aristotle left the school. We don't know why, but we can guess at some possibilities. Maybe it was because the Academy was putting too much emphasis on mathematics and pure theory and not enough on the practical sciences that interested Aristotle. The school passed into the hands of Plato's nephew, **Speusippus**, who was not distinguished.

ARISTOTLE MAY HAVE THOUGHT THAT HE SHOULD HAVE BEEN APPOINTED SUCCESSOR.

BUT THERE COULD ALSO HAVE BEEN A POLITICAL FACTOR INVOLVED.

Athens and Macedon were not on the best of terms because **Philip of Macedon**, Amyntas' successor, had recently sacked another Greek city. Aristotle might have been seen to be too pro-Macedonian. It may also have been the case that ownership of a school was possible only for citizens, and Aristotle was never an Athenian citizen.

Aristotle's Partners

Aristotle was away for twelve years. He went first to Atarneus, on the coast of Asia Minor, the other side of the Aegean Sea. The local ruler, or "tyrant" as they were called, was **Hermias**, who seems to have had some links with the Academy and who had fostered a small academic community under his protection. Hermias provided Aristotle and a friend, **Xenocrates**, who had gone with him with all that they needed.

THIS INCLUDED THE SMALL TOWN OF ASSOS TO LIVE IN.

WE WERE ABLE TO SPEND TIME IN TALKING, CONTEMPLATING AND PHILOSOPHISING.

Aristotle married Hermias' niece, **Pythias**, who bore him a daughter. They might have been in love.

In *The Politics*, which he may well have written at this time, he says that the ideal age for a man to marry was thirty-seven, and for a woman, eighteen. Since he was thirty-seven at the time, we may guess that Pythias was eighteen. He also strongly, and rather oddly, condemned adultery, calling it "disgraceful".

GREEK MARRIAGES WERE NORMALLY OF CONVENIENCE, FOR ESTABLISHING POLITICAL AND ECONOMIC LINKS AND FOR PRODUCING HEIRS.

IT WOULD BE CUSTOMARY FOR A MAN IN ARISTOTLE'S POSITION TO FIND SEXUAL SATISFACTION IN PROSTITUTES, CONCUBINES OR HETAIRAE ...

... WHO WERE RATHER LIKE JAPANESE GEISHAS.

Sadly, Pythias died. Aristotle later took another partner, called **Herpyllis**, who bore him a son, **Nicomachus**, who gave his name to *The Nicomachean Ethics*. We don't know whether they married. Aristotle died before Herpyllis. He was kind to her in his will, which remains. She was to be given away well, if she chose to re-marry.

I RECEIVED MONEY IN THE FORM OF SILVER, FIVE SERVANTS AND PROPERTY IN EITHER CHALCIS OR STAGIRA.

However, in a reminder that these were also brutal times, the city state of Atarneus was captured by the Persians in 341 BC and Hermias was tortured to death.

Gone Fishing

Just before this, Aristotle had moved away from Assos to the island of Lesbos and lived in the main city of Mytilene. There he met **Theophrastus**, who had been born on the island, and again set up a philosophical group similar to that at Assos.

He spent much of his time in and around a large sea lagoon that was mostly surrounded by land, an ideal place for specimens. Much of his work shows a keen appreciation of how living things work. His main method of explaining how things change, **teleology**, can be seen as having its origins in this giant rockpool.

13

Alexander the Great

In 343 BC came the invitation that history remembers. Philip of Macedon asked Aristotle to act as tutor to his thirteen year old son **Alexander**, who went on to conquer most of the known world during his short lifetime.

AS WITH PLATO, WE CAN BE SURE OF LITTLE OR NOTHING ABOUT THE RELATIONSHIP BETWEEN THE GREATEST MIND OF HIS TIME AND THE BOY WHO WAS TO BE THE GREATEST POWER.

ARISTOTLE'S EXISTING POLITICAL WRITINGS BETRAY NO PARTICULAR INTEREST IN THE MACEDONIAN EMPIRE.

There is nothing in Alexander's bloody career for which we can hold Aristotle responsible. Perhaps the most striking feature of the whole relationship was what little impact each had on the other.

Philip would have wanted the very best tutor for his son, and the existing family ties from their fathers' days must have pointed unmistakably at Aristotle. Perhaps Aristotle tried to combine the classical virtues of the heroes of Homer's *Iliad* with the most recent thinking on ethics and politics. He was convinced of the superiority of the Greeks.

I REGARD ALL NON-GREEKS AS BARBARIANS ...

WOULD THIS VIEW - TYPICAL OF **ALL** GREEKS - HAVE ENCOURAGED ME TO CONQUER AND DOMINATE THEM?

This seems to have been only partly effective. Alexander chose a Persian wife and strongly encouraged intermarriage among his troops. Aristotle would certainly have disapproved of this. Alexander may also have arranged to have animals and plants sent back to Aristotle from the conquered lands.

The Return to Athens

Philip was killed in 346 BC and Alexander had no more time for school. Aristotle stayed in Stagira for a while and then left northern Greece the next year to return to Athens. Although his association with Alexander gave him security and prosperity in Athens, the relationship may have ended on a sour note. Aristotle's nephew, **Callisthenes**, had been appointed as the official historian of the conquests. Alexander, becoming increasingly paranoid, charged him with treason.

I INCARCERATED HIM IN A TRAVELLING CAGE AND THEN EXECUTED HIM.

It is possible that Alexander also contemplated a similar fate for Aristotle as a relative of Callisthenes, but, fortunately, nothing came of it.

Aristotle Founds the Lyceum

Aristotle was almost fifty years old when he returned to Athens, a mature and respected philosopher. The leadership of the Academy was again vacant at this time, following the death of **Speusippus**, but Aristotle was not appointed. He seems not to have been prepared to work under his old colleague **Xenocrates**, and opened his own school, the Lyceum.

IT WAS SITUATED JUST OUTSIDE ATHENS NEXT TO THE TEMPLE OF APOLLO LYCEUS, AN AREA WHICH WAS A HAUNT OF PHILOSOPHERS EVEN BEFORE THIS.

THE ARCHAEOLOGICAL REMAINS OF THE LYCEUM HAVE RECENTLY BEEN DISCOVERED UNDER THE STREETS OF MODERN ATHENS.

17

The Peripatetics

It was here, at the Lyceum, that Aristotle lived and worked for the next twelve years, overseeing the work of scholars and researchers and providing teaching. He taught in the covered walkway of the building, called the *peripatos* in Greek.

The school had a very wide range of interests, but tended to specialize in history and biology.

"Sinning Twice"

In 323 BC, Alexander the Great died. The Macedonian Empire, which Alexander held together, began to disintegrate. The Athenians seized the opportunity and tried to break free of Macedon. Aristotle was in danger. His Macedonian links were well-known and he was a friend of the Macedonian Regent of Athens. A trumped up charge of impiety (disrespect for the Gods) was brought against him, as it had before against **Socrates**. He left Athens.

I SHALL DENY THE ATHENIANS THE OPPORTUNITY OF **SINNING TWICE** AGAINST PHILOSOPHY.

SOCRATES WAS CONDEMNED TO DEATH FOR IMPIETY IN 399 BC.

Evidence of a True Story

This story may not, of course, be true. However, there is another story about this troubled time for Aristotle, for which we have independent evidence. It is said that he wrote to the Macedonian Regent, **Antipater**, saying: "As for the honour which was voted me at Delphi and of which I have now been stripped, I am neither greatly concerned nor greatly unconcerned."

The End

His last journey was from Athens to Chalcis, on the island of Euboea, where his mother had property. He died a year or so later, in 322 BC, from some kind of stomach complaint. There is an alternative version of his death which I would like to believe. The sea channel between the island of Euboea and the mainland is very narrow. Although there are virtually no tides in the Mediterranean as a whole, there are very complicated tides in this channel.

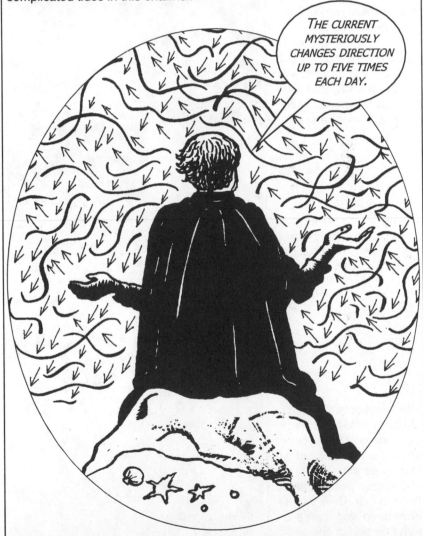

THE CURRENT MYSTERIOUSLY CHANGES DIRECTION UP TO FIVE TIMES EACH DAY.

It is said that Aristotle died of frustration trying to puzzle out the reasons for this constant oscillation.

A Good Man

All that we know of Aristotle indicates that he was a good man, both kindly and generous. His character does appear to be like that of "the good man" that he writes about in his ethical works. Some have described him, because of his writings, as pompous and humourless, but this has more to do with the way that his writings have been used than with what he said.

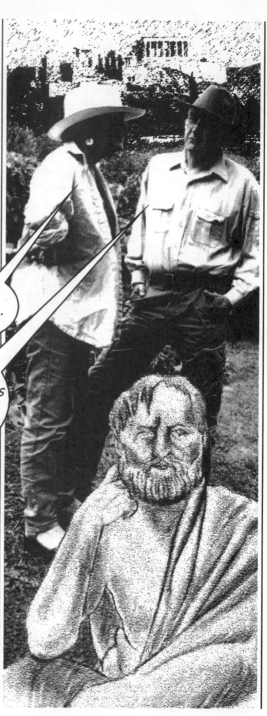

HE HAD ENEMIES ...

THEY DESCRIBED HIM AS HAVING SPINDLY LEGS AND SMALL EYES, AND SAID HE SPOKE WITH A LISP.

The busts of him, which probably date from the early years of the Lyceum, show a sharp-featured and rather aristocratic man, with a beard and full head of hair. He is said to have been well-dressed, with fine cloaks and sandals, and to have worn rings.

His Writings

We have only a third of Aristotle's work. The rest is lost. Thirty books remain, or about 2,000 modern pages. He wrote and published many works intended for popular consumption, which he called the *"exoterics"*, in the literary style of his time, poetry, letters, essays and dialogues. These are said to have been beautifully written. **Cicero** has left us a description of them.

We don't know where they went, but perhaps some of them were destroyed in the anti-Macedonian times that followed the death of Alexander.

Lecture Notes

The works that we do have do not demonstrate much of a literary style. They were never published during his lifetime and survived his death. They are spare and difficult, with repetitions, abrupt and unexplained transitions and connections, and little in the way of decoration or jokes. The poet **Thomas Gray** said that reading Aristotle was like eating dried hay. This is something of an exaggeration, but his writing can be hard work. It is generally agreed that these *"esoteric"* (or *"acroatic"*) works are actually lecture notes, the working documents that he used on a daily basis for his teaching.

Also, lecture notes tend to be used for years, with new bits being included and the old bits which they replace – and with which they disagree – not always erased.

Aristotle's philosophical method was to find a puzzle in the area that he was investigating, called an *aporia*, then work through to a solution.

Also, they may not all be the work of Aristotle. Some may have been taken down by students during or after lectures, perhaps inaccurately. Later editors may have inserted passages or changed parts that they felt were mistakes. The works are known as *treatises*, and it is likely that Aristotle's papers were gathered together and put into these treatises by others.

History of Aristotle's Works

The story has it that Theophrastus inherited all of Aristotle's papers on the latter's death.

They were finally edited and published by the last head of the Lyceum, **Andronicus** of Rhodes. The standard Greek version of Aristotle's works used today, that produced by **Immanuel Bekker** in 1831, is based on Andronicus.

SO THE TITLES AND THE ORDERING – AND WHO KNOWS WHAT ELSE OF THE WORKS – WE OWE TO ANDRONICUS WHO PRODUCED HIS VERSION THREE HUNDRED YEARS AFTER ARISTOTLE'S DEATH.

WE THEREFORE HAVE NO KNOWLEDGE OF THE SEQUENCE IN WHICH ARISTOTLE WROTE HIS WORKS, AND CAN SAY LITTLE ABOUT HIS INTELLECTUAL DEVELOPMENT.

There is a small academic industry attempting to establish whether he began as a Platonist and moved to his own distinctive brand of empiricism over his lifetime, or whether the reverse was the case. The major difference between the works as Aristotle wrote them and Andronicus' version is that the originals probably consisted of a great many short treatises. Andronicus grouped them together on the basis of some general topic.

The Arab Connection

When Rome fell, knowledge of almost all of Aristotle's work and thought was lost to Western Europe.

The Works

The works, as they appear in Bekker's *Aristotle*, are as follows.
Those thought not to have been written by Aristotle are marked with an asterisk. Parts of other works are probably not by him either.

Categories
de Interpretatione
Prior Analytics
Posterior Analytics
Topics
Sophistical Refutations
Physics
On the Heavens
On Generation and Corruption
Meteorology
*On the Universe
On the Soul
Sense and Sensibilia
On Memory
On Sleep
On Dreams
On Divination in Sleep
On Length and Shortness of Life
On Youth, Old Age, Life and Death
On respiration
*On Breath
History of Animals
Parts of Animals
Movement of Animals

Progression of Animals
Generation of Animals
*On Colours
*On Things Heard
*Physiognomonics
*On Plants
*On Marvellous Things Heard
*Mechanics
*Problems
*On Invisible Lines
*The Situations and Names of Winds
On Melissus, Xenophanes and Gorgias
Metaphysics
Nicomachean Ethics
*Magna Moralia
Eudemian Ethics
*On Virtues and Vices
Politics
*Economics
Rhetoric
*Rhetoric to Alexander
Poetics

Metaphysics, the Study of Ultimate Reality

Many would say that Aristotle's metaphysics are his greatest achievement. Their influence has certainly been enormous. The central thrust of the writings is that the world exists as it seems to exist, and can be understood by ordinary people with the right abilities and training. The scientific world view has its roots in this work. Indeed, it is difficult to see how science could be done at all without this particular insight.

Realist and Relativists

When Aristotle began to ask awkward questions about reality, he found himself in an argument with an oddly contemporary ring. Can the external world be described objectively, as it really is, or are all our descriptions of the world rooted in our own personal experience? We can describe the argument as between the **realists** and the **relativists** (or anti-realists). Today similar debates go on between scientists, who are the realists, and postmodernists, who are the relativists. **The Eleatic School**, which was influential in Athens at the time, held that the world was fundamentally unknowable by humans.

These views were to give rise to the **Sophist** movement, to which Socrates, Plato and Aristotle were deeply opposed, because the Sophists rejected the idea of ultimate truth.

The Eleatic View of Monism

The way in which Aristotle and the Eleatics discussed these issues seems strange to us because the terms they use no longer seem relevant. However, one of the main reasons for this seeming irrelevance today is that Aristotle's arguments were so effective. Eleatics were followers of **Parmenides**, who took the **monist** view that the world consisted only of one unchanging thing.

THE ELEATICS HAVE A PROFOUNDLY UNSCIENTIFIC LACK OF FAITH IN THE NORMAL CONCEPTS OF CHANGE, TIME, SPACE AND THE DIFFERENCES BETWEEN THINGS.

THEY ALSO TEND TO BE MISCHIEVOUS IN ARGUMENT AND EVEN CLAIM THAT IN THE END ALL ARGUMENT IS FUTILE.

Zeno of Elea (495?-435? BC) developed a number of paradoxes that are still puzzling today, and which seem to show that neither time nor motion is possible.

Achilles and the Tortoise

One of Zeno's paradoxes features the legendary warrior **Achilles** in a race against a tortoise. He gives the tortoise a good start and begins to run. But, the paradox is, can he ever catch up with it?

EACH TIME ACHILLES REACHES THE POINT WHERE THE TORTOISE WAS ...

... IT HAS MOVED TO THE NEXT POINT, AND SO ON ...

ACHILLES CAN GET CLOSER TO THE TORTOISE BUT NEVER REACH OR OVERTAKE IT.

What does the paradox suggest? We know that Achilles, in reality, can overtake the tortoise, and so there **must** be a finite "chunk" of space and time. Space and time cannot be infinitely divisible.

Time and the Arrow

Another paradox suggests that an arrow in flight is actually **at rest**. It occupies at any one instant in time a space that is exactly identical to its own shape.

If space and time are made up of indivisible finite units, then we are faced with the paradox of a length or duration that cannot be divided. If they are infinitely divisible, how can any number of infinitely small things make something that is big? Zeno's conclusion is that neither time nor motion are real, that a "changing world" is an illusion, since change is impossible. Aristotle had to resolve such arguments to supply a scientific explanation of the world as it really appears.

Plato's Ideal Forms

Although Plato was opposed to the Eleatic position, his own unchanging realm of the **Ideal Forms** demonstrates its influence on him. Plato did see the ordinary, everyday world as inferior and illusory. For him, the things that really existed were the forms. These were rather like perfect and eternal templates from which were copied all of the things that we see around us. The forms were not physical, whereas the copies were.

THEREFORE THE NON-PHYSICAL IS "REAL" AND THE PHYSICAL "UNREAL".

ARISTOTLE'S ARGUMENTS AGAINST THIS POSITION ARE DESIGNED TO SHOW THAT CHANGE IS A REAL FEATURE OF REAL THINGS.

REAL THINGS, SUCH AS TREES AND GOATS, ARE THE FUNDAMENTAL AND ONLY THINGS THAT FULLY EXIST.

Ultimate Reality

The issue was concerned with both **what** exists (ontology) and the extent to which we can **know** what exists (epistemology). Aristotle understood that an adequate response to the powerful Eleatic arguments would need to provide answers to both of these questions and, while they cannot be separated entirely, they would need to be approached differently. He dealt with the epistemological question with his conception of scientific method. However, the ontological question required an exercise in metaphysics.

METAPHYSICS IS SEEN TODAY AS THE STUDY OF "ULTIMATE REALITY", OF WHATEVER EXISTS BEYOND OR BEHIND THAT WHICH WE CAN STUDY WITH ORDINARY SCIENCE.

HOWEVER, FOR ME, IT WAS TO BE THE BASIS FOR SCIENCE.

The word itself is now very common in Philosophy, but it originally just meant "after physics". The story is that Andronicus was puzzled by this particular collection of writings and was not sure how to file them, so he put them on the shelf "after" the physics writings.

35

Empiricism: the Basis of Science

Aristotle realized that if there is a world, and if the world is to be comprehensible to us, then we have to have full knowledge of what it is that is **in** the world. It is as if the world is a box filled with things, or **substances**, to use Aristotle's word.

DISCUSSION OF THE BOX ITSELF, WHILE IGNORING THE CONTENTS, WAS TO PUT THE ARGUMENT THE WRONG WAY ROUND.

WHEN WE HAVE EXPLAINED EVERYTHING THAT IS IN THE BOX, WE HAVE COMPLETE KNOWLEDGE OF THE WORLD. THERE IS NO BOX.

In this we can see the beginnings of the philosophical tradition of empiricism.

The Middle Way

While Aristotle seems to have almost intuitively rejected the Eleatic and Sophist denial of the possibility of explanation of the world, he also seems to have recognized that there were pitfalls in explanation itself. At one extreme, Plato sought to explain the world in a dualist way: two realms, one more "real" than the other. This kind of explanation seems to be almost mystical in its reliance on non-physical entities.

BUT THE IMPOSSIBILITY OF OBSERVING CERTAINLY DID.

THE FACT THAT THE ENTITIES WERE NOT PHYSICAL MAY NOT HAVE BOTHERED ARISTOTLE ...

AT THE OTHER EXTREME IS **REDUCTIONISM.**

ANY EXPLANATION OF ANYTHING IS ONLY COMPLETE WHEN IT IS REDUCED OR ANALYSED TO ITS SMALLEST COMPONENT PARTS.

Democritus and **Leucippus** believed that these parts were **atoms** – small indivisible balls. This might be fine in explaining a piece of paper, but less useful in explaining the letter from the bank that was written on it. Aristotle wanted to find a middle way, avoiding both mysticism and reductionism.

37

Definitions and Descriptions

Aristotle also realized that we would need to make a careful distinction between a **description** of something and its **definition**. He believed that when we describe something we are not really saying anything about what it really is, we are simply marking it off from other things. An explanation of the **real** nature of something must entail some sort of convincing definition, rather than just a description.

IF I SAY THAT I AM BALDING OR FORGETFUL, I AM INDEED SAYING USEFUL, DESCRIPTIVE THINGS.

*BUT I AM NOT SAYING ANYTHING ABOUT THE REAL ME, THE **ESSENCE** OF ME.*

It might be thought that I could accomplish this by saying all the possible things that could be said about myself by way of description, that this would be "all of me". However, it is difficult to see where this list would end. Also, descriptions do tend to be relative, to depend on the point of view of the describer. This argument would leave us in much the same position as the Eleatics and the Sophists.

Ontology: the Essential Quality

Therefore, thought Aristotle, we need to be able to identify an essential quality of something, some absolutely central feature that makes it **what it is** – its ontology – rather than simply marking it off from other things. So, in my case, apart from being balding and forgetful, I am also something else, something that makes me human – a thing with a **human nature**.

THAT "HUMAN NATURE" WOULD BE A DEFINITION.

THEREFORE, THE TASK OF METAPHYSICS IS TO EXPLAIN HOW THINGS EXIST THROUGH THIS ESSENTIAL AND CENTRAL ASPECT THAT THEY HAVE.

What is "Is"?

Aristotle begins *The Categories*, in a very characteristic way, by trying to work out the meaning of the verb "to be". When we say that something *exists*, what do we mean by that term? Aristotle thought that ordinary language does actually reflect the way in which the world is put together.

LANGUAGE AND THE WORLD MIRROR EACH OTHER, THAT IS TO SAY, THEY ARE ISOMORPHIC.

HOWEVER, WE OFTEN USE LANGUAGE BADLY, WHICH CONFUSES US AND GIVES RISE TO PHILOSOPHICAL DIFFICULTIES.

IN SOME WAYS, THIS VIEW IS SIMILAR TO THAT OF TWENTIETH-CENTURY LINGUISTIC PHILOSOPHERS.

FOR EXAMPLE, IF WE LOOK AT TWO SENTENCES ...

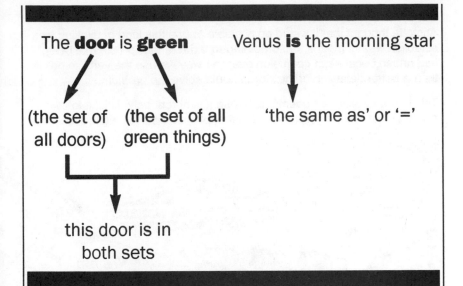

The **door** is **green**

Venus **is** the morning star

(the set of all doors)   (the set of all green things)

'the same as' or '='

this door is in both sets

We can see that both sentences contain the word "is", part of the verb "to be". We might assume that it functions in the same way in both sentences. However, it does not. In sentence 1, it tells us that the door has a particular property, that of greenness. In sentence 2, however, it is doing something quite different.

*IT IS TELLING US THAT ONE PHYSICAL OBJECT HAS TWO DIFFERENT **NAMES.***

IN MODERN LOGIC, THE WORD WOULD BE EXPRESSED AS TWO DISTINCT AND DIFFERENT SYMBOLS.

"The door is green" might be expressed using the idea of the set of all doors and the set of all green things. This door is in both sets. Here the two sets intersect, usually shown as an inverted U. "Venus is the morning star" would use notation indicating "is the same as", usually shown as "=". Aristotle himself did not disentangle this particular case, but it is a good example of how we can confuse ourselves by using language carelessly.

Existence: the Problem of Being

Aristotle thought that it would be possible to use this kind of thinking to establish what it means for something to **exist**. If the "problem of being" had arisen because of confusion over the way we use the verb "to be", then a better definition of the word should solve the problem.

This is not as silly as it seems, because it is notoriously difficult to explain what "existing" refers to. Most explanations are tautologous.

FOR EXAMPLE, WE COULD SAY THAT "TO EXIST" MEANS "TO HAVE AN INSTANCE", BUT THIS REALLY GETS US NO FURTHER FORWARD ...

THE TWO TERMS MEAN THE SAME THING.

Other approaches have suggested that the best way to explain existence is to say that an object exists when it has an effect, either directly or indirectly, on an **observer**. However, this was just the kind of argument Aristotle would have wanted to avoid.

IT MEANS THAT FOR SOMETHING TO EXIST REQUIRES ALSO THE EXISTENCE OF AN OBSERVER.

THIS APPROACH LATER DEVELOPED INTO THE PHILOSOPHICAL TRADITION OF IDEALISM ...

But, at the time this would have struck Aristotle as being very similar to the views of the Sophists, and therefore wrong and dangerous. As the Sophist **Protagoras** said: "Man is the measure of all things." If man were necessary for the very existence of all things, then he would certainly have their measure.

Genus and Species

So Aristotle's idea of approaching the problem through definition was probably as good a way forward as was available to him. He began the task by describing how the process of definition works in general. First of all, things can be divided into groups according to what kinds of things they are (*genera*). Within these groups, further sub-divisions can be made according to distinguishing features that are unique.

TO FIND A DEFINITION OF AN OAK TREE, ONE MUST FIRST OF ALL ESTABLISH THAT IT IS A MEMBER OF THE GENUS "PLANT".

ONE MIGHT THEN ASK: "IS IT LARGE OR SMALL? DO THE LEAVES COME OFF IT IN WINTER?"

An oak tree could then at least partly be defined as a large, deciduous plant. The full definition would be the "species". The way in which we classify living things today with long Latin names can be traced directly back to Aristotle's technique here.

It follows from this method of definition that the same word will often apply to two different things. "Plant" is quite rightly part of the definition of both an oak tree and a daisy. The two are synonymous.

THEY BOTH REFER TO THE SAME THING, THE GENUS "PLANT", ALTHOUGH THERE ARE DIFFERENCES BETWEEN THEM.

We would probably have no difficulty with this. However, he wants to go further; he wants to say that the synonymity is **in** the objects, not just in the way we talk about them. They have "plantness". In this way, he believes, we can use definitions of things to find out what they really are.

45

Thisness

Aristotle thought that the fundamental things that exist, that **be**, in the world are particular individual entities, such as my cat, that tree, this particular person. These are ontologically basic. They are **substances** (*ousia*). The other things that exist in the world are, in a variety of ways, secondary to these. Substances, sometimes known as **particulars**, are those things that we have direct personal experience of. As he said …

... THEY HAVE THE QUALITY OF **THISNESS**. BUT TO HAVE EXPERIENCE **ONLY** OF THESE WOULD BE EXTRAORDINARILY LIMITING.

OUR LIVES WOULD BE LIKE THOSE OF ANIMALS, A MASS OF SENSATION AND A FLEETING HAZE OF MEMORY.

To have knowledge beyond this, scientific knowledge (*episteme*), we need to know about **universals**, things that are in a number of different particular substances. For example, a particular might be this white piece of paper, a universal would be the whiteness that is in many pieces of paper.

Thisness Is Not An Illusion

Aristotle sees the primary particular things of the world fitting into more general classifications that are less important than the particular because they depend on them for their existence. Using his terminology, we can "say of" Socrates that he is a human. This is a definition.

IF WE SAY THAT SOCRATES IS HONOURABLE, WE ARE SAYING THAT THE HONOUR IS "IN" HIM. THIS IS A DESCRIPTION.

*IT IS SAYING SOMETHING ABOUT A PARTICULAR THING, **A SUBSTANCE.***

The distinction may seem unimportant or even artificial today, but it was of major significance for Aristotle because it provided a powerful argument against the Eleatics. When we say that a characteristic is "in" a substance, it is not, therefore, in the observer. It is not variable or relative to the person **observing**, it is objectively **there**, in the thing. It is not an **illusion**.

The Categories

What sorts of things can be "in" a substance? Aristotle answers this question with his well-known list of the **Categories**. This is a classification of the ways in which a substance can **be**. To grasp his point here we need to recap on some basic grammar. A great many sentences in language are of the form **subject-predicate**. That is to say, they have a subject, which the sentence is about, and a predicate which tells us something about the subject. "The door" – subject – "is green" – predicate.

THE MISTAKE THAT THE ELEATICS MAKE IS TO FAIL TO REALIZE THAT THE SUBJECT AND THE PREDICATE DO DIFFERENT JOBS IN LANGUAGE.

IF BOTH ARE TREATED AS SUBJECTS, THEN WE ARE TREATING BOTH AS NAMES, AND THERE IS NO CONNECTION BETWEEN THEM.

In the sentence "Venus is the morning star" the two names are interchangeable, but neither tells us anything about the "substance" that they are referring to. This is fine for this sentence, but won't work with "The door is brown". To treat "is brown" as a name would be to say that all descriptions are just names, and names are linguistic options. We would be back in the world of illusions.

Aristotle and My Cat

So predicates must be something else. They need to be in the world as well as in language. They must be things "in" substances. The categories are the various ways in which predicates are in substances. The first category is **substance** itself, and it is by far the most important. Also significant are **quality**, **quantity** and **relation**, followed by **time**, **place**, **position**, **state**, **activity** and **passivity**. A substance will be a member of a species – say, my cat Angus. His quality would be "tabby", his quantity, two kilos, and his relation would be "mine" or "my other cat". The other categories are really developments of these last three, but in this case the time may be "nine p.m.", the place may be "by the fire", the position is "curled up", the state is certainly "greedy", the activity is "purring" and the passivity is "being stroked".

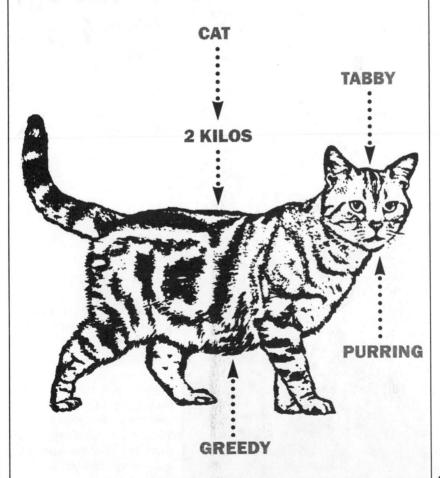

CAT

TABBY

2 KILOS

PURRING

GREEDY

Are the Categories Real?

All substances – objects in the world – will have something to be said about them under most of these ten categories. Some authorities say, quite plausibly, that the nine categories that follow substance match the kinds of question we could ask about a substance other than its definition.

IN RETROSPECT, MOST PHILOSOPHERS REMAIN UNCONVINCED THAT ARISTOTLE'S CATEGORIES ARE REAL ...

SUBSTANCE QUALITY QUANTITY RELATION TIME PLACE POSITION STATE ACTIVITY PASSIVITY

RATHER THAN SIMPLY ABOUT THE WAY THAT WE USE WORDS AND EXPRESSIONS.

Nevertheless, all other philosophers since Aristotle who have attempted to achieve the same result – a clear picture of the world as it is – have come up against similar problems.

Science and the Categories

Aristotle thought that science can go beyond these categories. These are about the immediate objects of sensation. When we do science, we need to be more abstract and general. To do this, we need a classification of the definitions of substances rather than the descriptions. These are the things that can be "said of" something rather than the things that are "in" something. We say of Socrates that he is a human, therefore "human" is a general term that is derived from separate people, it is a **species**. Then again, people are all animals, like dogs and goats, so the term "animal" is an even more general term derived from "human", "goat" and "dog". It is a **genus**.

human

goat

dog

THE INTELLECTUAL ACTIVITY OF SCIENCE IS ABOUT THE PROCESS BY WHICH WE MAP OUT THIS HIERARCHY OF DEFINITIONS.

Each level of definition is more general and more inclusive. The highest and most general classification of definition is that of substance itself, because all particular things are substances.

Individual Substances

However, the term "substance" is not very informative – it gives little of the detail of definition. In fact, the lower down in the hierarchy you go, the more information you get. Aristotle believed that "species" was the most informative term of classification. To say "Socrates was a human" tells us much more than that he was an animal (although he was, as well). That he was a human reveals to us the essential nature of Socrates the individual.

THE LESS GENERAL YOU GET, THE MORE SUBSTANTIAL IS YOUR DEFINITION.

NATURAL LIVING CREATURES, SUCH AS SOCRATES, OR THAT GOAT OR THAT TREE, ARE THE MOST BASIC SUBSTANCES IN THE WORLD.

The more general classifications cannot exist without individual substances. This might seem blindingly obvious to many of us today, but we need to remember that he was arguing against the Eleatics, who didn't really believe in individual substances at all.

Universals

These terms, species, genus and so on, refer to **universals**. As with the categories, there is a problem about what universals actually are. The problem is that while he wants to say that they are real, they cannot be physical. An individual dog is physical, so are all the dogs in the world – even all the dogs that ever have been or will be, in a way. But the concept of "dog" is not.

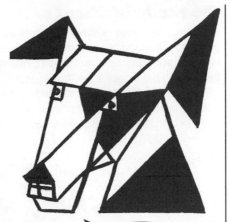

SO, IF IT IS NOT PHYSICAL, IS IT NEVERTHELESS REAL?

ARISTOTLE IS AMBIVALENT. MAYBE HE DID NOT SEE IT AS A SIGNIFICANT PROBLEM.

ALTHOUGH IT IS MORE LIKELY THAT HE HAD NO CLEAR ANSWER.

After all, it is over just this kind of problem that argument rages today between scientists and postmodernists. However, Aristotle did feel that his arguments for the categories were sufficiently strong to deal with the Platonic forms. What Plato had done was to confuse categories. When Plato said that there was a perfect version of beauty existing eternally in some non-physical realm, this was to see beauty as a **subject** rather than a predicate, as **substance** rather than quality.

The Kinds of Change

How then do these primary substances – the most basic of things –
change? This was a key question, because if there was a world of
material substances, then they obviously did change. The Eleatics said
that change is impossible, but Aristotle argued that it was possible to
explain both **how** things changed and **why** they changed. The former
answer rests on his conception of **substance** and the **categories**.
The second answer rests with his conception of **cause**.

*THERE SEEMS
TO BE **TWO KINDS** OF
CHANGE, BOTH OF WHICH
NEED A "HOW" AND A
"WHY" ANSWER.*

In the first case some substance changes some aspect of its character.

A human becomes older, a tree loses its leaves.

Aristotle says that the substance, the human or the tree, is experiencing a transformation in some or other of its categories, those things that are qualities of it but that are separate from its essence.

AN OLDER HUMAN IS STILL A HUMAN. A TREE WITHOUT LEAVES REMAINS A TREE.

IN THE SECOND CASE, SOMETHING COMES TO BE OUT OF NOTHING.

TO USE A FAVOURITE EXAMPLE OF ARISTOTLE, ONE DAY THERE IS NOTHING, THEN A FEW DAYS LATER THERE IS A STATUE.

WHERE HAS IT COME FROM?

This is a more difficult problem, and his answer marks the first appearance of his conception of substance as a combination of **form** and **matter**.

Form and Matter

In the case of the human becoming older, the human continues. But in the case of the bronze statue, what is it that continues? What is it that the statue is **from**? Aristotle's answer is **matter**. We might at this point conclude that he is now saying that there is something that is more basic than substance, namely matter. But he is not. Matter is only that out of which substances come. It is not basic. It is amorphous and characterless.

The form is put into the matter to produce the substance, the statue. In the case of an oak tree, which comes into existence from an acorn, the form is intrinsic to the acorn and the oak tree. The acorn automatically puts the form of the tree into the crude matter of soil and water, because it is in its "nature" to do so.

Teleology: Arguing from Design or Purpose

So, Aristotle sees substances as characterized by a purpose or design. In the case of the statue, we see the purpose of the sculptor, and in the case of the tree, the intrinsic purpose of the acorn. In the case of the acorn, the form is internal. While in the case of the sculpture, the form is externally applied by the sculptor.

THIS MAKES NATURAL THINGS LIKE THE TREE MORE BASIC THAN ARTIFICIAL THINGS LIKE THE SCULPTURE.

*BELIEF IN DESIGN MAKES HIM A **TELEOLOGIST** ...*

SOMEONE WHO EXPLAINS THINGS BY REFERENCE TO THEIR PURPOSE.

Thinking of this kind leads to problems, but is an effective explanation of **how** things change. | 57

Ancient and Modern Reductionism

But **why** do they change? Even if the world is made of many different things, why don't they just stay as they are? Aristotle has, of course, already partly answered the question by saying that some kinds of transformation, perhaps all kinds, are purposeful and relate to form. However, this is not quite enough. Some philosophers, such as the pre-Socratic Atomists, would argue that all this talk of "form" is irrelevant.

*A CHANGE IN SOMETHING CAN BE EXPLAINED ENTIRELY BY **REDUCING** OUR EXPLANATION TO THE MOST BASIC MATERIAL LEVEL.*

*IN THE END, WE CAN EXPLAIN THE WAY A TREE LOSES ITS LEAVES OR A HUMAN GROWS OLD BY LOOKING AT THE UNDERLYING NATURE OF THE **PARTICLES** THAT MAKE UP THE TREE AND THE HUMAN.*

Aristotle's View of Cause

Aristotle was deeply opposed to any such reductionist kind of explanation, and wanted to find explanations for change at the level of the substance – the thing itself – rather than at the level of its constituent parts, because substance was "basic". To do this, he needed to explain things in terms of purposes, as well as **causes** in our modern sense. A contemporary causal explanation always puts the cause of something before the event that we are seeking to explain.

WHEN I PUMP UP A BICYCLE TYRE, THE AIR IN IT (AND THE END OF THE PUMP) GETS HOT, **BECAUSE** I INCREASE THE PRESSURE.

THIS IS AN EXAMPLE OF THE WORKING OF BOYLE'S LAW, WHICH SAYS THAT CHANGES IN THE PRESSURE OF A GAS WILL CAUSE CHANGES IN THE TEMPERATURE.

ROBERT BOYLE

Teleological explanations place the cause of an event **after** the event we are seeking to explain. They involve a discussion of purpose.

FOR EXAMPLE, I DRIVE TO THE CITY IN ORDER TO VISIT THE THEATRE.

TO EXPLAIN THE DRIVE, I IDENTIFY THE **CAUSE** AS A THEATRE VISIT THAT TAKES PLACE **AFTER** THE DRIVE.

The Nature of Change

Aristotle puts the concept of "nature" at the centre of his teleological method of explaining change. He says that this nature has to do with the form of a substance rather than its matter. This is best seen in the case of a living creature or plant. It is in the nature of a tree to spread its branches upwards and dig its roots deep.

Taken together, their self-generation and their characteristic behaviour will be their nature. This idea of Aristotle's would form a good basis for contemporary ecological thinking. Plants and animals all have their own nature and we should not interfere with them.

Aition or "Type of Explanation"

Aristotle does not, of course, deny that cause in our modern sense exists. He just thinks that this kind of cause will not give us an adequate or full explanation of why things change.

IN **THE PHYSICS**, I PRESENT MY FAMOUS LIST OF CAUSES WHICH PROVIDE A FULL AND COMPLETE EXPLANATION.

THE GREEK WORD FOR CAUSE IS **"AITION"**, AND THIS CAN BE MISLEADING.

IN THE CONTEXT OF **THE PHYSICS**, IT IS PROBABLY BETTER TO READ **AITION** AS MEANING "TYPE OF EXPLANATION".

The four causes that he gives are the ways in which some object or event or state of affairs can be made to make sense.

The Four Causes

The first is the **material cause**. As its name suggests, this explanation concerns the matter from which something is formed.

A PIECE OF PAPER WILL BURN BECAUSE THAT IS WHAT THE MATTER THAT THE PIECE OF PAPER IS CONSTRUCTED FROM IS LIKE. IT IS FLAMMABLE.

The second is the **formal cause**. Something changes in a particular way because of the pattern or form it needs to fulfil its purpose.

A CATERPILLAR TRANSFORMS ITSELF SO THAT IT CAN BECOME, PHYSICALLY, A BUTTERFLY.

The third is the **efficient cause**. This is usually said to correspond most closely with our modern version of cause. It refers to the factor or event that is the specific origin of the change.

IT IS THAT WHICH CAN BE PINPOINTED IN **TIME** AS BRINGING ABOUT THE TRANSFORMATION, SUCH AS THE LIGHTNING STRIKE THAT BRINGS DOWN THE TREE.

The fourth is the **final cause**. This is the most controversial of Aristotle's causes. It explains a change in terms of the **final purpose** of something, that for which it was designed. As we have seen, this works well for living creatures. The salmon swims up the river to the spawning grounds because, well, that's what salmon do, finally (in more ways than one).

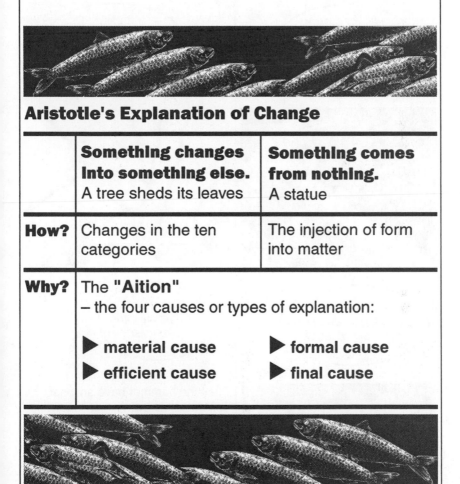

Aristotle's Explanation of Change

	Something changes into something else. A tree sheds its leaves	**Something comes from nothing.** A statue
How?	Changes in the ten categories	The injection of form into matter
Why?	The **"Aition"** – the four causes or types of explanation: ▶ **material cause** ▶ **efficient cause**	▶ **formal cause** ▶ **final cause**

The Problem of Purpose

Problems do arise in the case of non-living artefacts. We can easily understand the final purpose of a hammer, to drive in nails. But why does the hammer fall and hit my toe when tipped from the bench?

> THE MATERIAL CAUSE OF THIS EVENT IS THE WEIGHTY NATURE OF THE TOOL.

> THE FORMAL CAUSE IS THE SHAPE IT NEEDS TO BE USEFUL.

> THE EFFICIENT CAUSE IS THE ACCIDENTAL PUSH FROM MY ELBOW.

> BUT WHAT IS THE FINAL CAUSE IN THIS CASE?

Does the hammer have an inner purpose of its own, which is to go **downwards**? Aristotle would probably answer yes, that most things share, as at least part of their final purpose, a "going-down-wardness", a desire to reach the lowest point possible. This may seem very odd to us now, but then the Greeks had no knowledge of gravity.

Emergent Features

In Aristotle's four causes, we can see two underlying perspectives, which are both kinds of scientific explanation and, at the same time, features of the world. On the one hand, we have a material, mechanical world of necessity.

The way in which things are organized and constructed (either by us or by themselves) leads to the emergence of **new features** or character-istics which can **only** be related to the organization of the thing.

Natural Things and Artefacts

Perhaps Aristotle fails to distinguish between artefacts and natural things, between things that are made and things that make themselves. However, he really did think that the obviously useful nature of the various parts of animals ...

... THE FINS OF FISH FOR EXAMPLE ...

*... ARE NOT JUST **LIKE** THINGS THAT WERE MADE BY HUMANS BUT IN PRINCIPLE **THE SAME AS** ARTEFACTS.*

He thought that the formal and final causes were not just a way of explaining natural things, but were real features of natural things and the way that they change.

The Problem of Form

While in many ways satisfying, the conclusions that Aristotle comes to in *The Physics* leave important issues unresolved. In particular, what is the correct relationship between form and matter in substance? He seems to suggest that a substance, such as a tree, is an uneasy bond of specific physical matter and non-physical general form. Which comes first? Which gives substance its nature?

MUCH OF THE REASONING THAT HE HAS EMPLOYED SUGGESTS THAT THE ANSWER IS FORM.

HOWEVER, THIS WOULD LEAVE HIM WITH A BIG PROBLEM ...

AND I AM AWARE OF IT.

The Metaphysical Solution

Form is, indeed, general. Formal properties are those properties shared by a number of substances and therefore do not have a particular concrete character. They are **"said of"** particular substances, they are not **"in"** them. But they are real.

*IN **THE CATEGORIES,** HE SAID THAT PRIORITY MUST BE GIVEN TO THE PARTICULARS, THE REAL **PHYSICAL** THINGS IN THE WORLD.*

THEY ARE THE MOST BASIC OF THINGS.

*IS HE NOW SAYING THAT **NON-PHYSICAL FORM** IS MORE BASIC?*

*THE TASK OF HIS GREAT WORK, **THE METAPHYSICS,** IS TO SOLVE THIS PROBLEM.*

Without a solution his whole enterprise, the establishment of science, is in jeopardy. The argument is dense and difficult, and scholars are by no means in agreement about what he said or what he meant.

Basic Species

One answer is to move away from his original position, which was to say that individual substances, the actual things in the world, are basic. The advantage of this is that the subject matter of science is clear – "things in the world". The disadvantage is that unless he can clarify the relationship between the form and the matter of these things, we don't know what they are.

IN BOOK ZETA OF **THE METAPHYSICS,** HE TRIES TO SOLVE THE PROBLEM BY CHANGING THIS VIEW AND CLAIMING INSTEAD THAT PARTICULAR SUBSTANCES ARE NOT BASIC.

I SUGGEST THAT "SPECIES" ARE BASIC - SUCH AS THE SPECIES OF HUMANS OR OF CHAIRS.

He believed that all that could be said of a species was **definition**, there was no description. Here, matter and form are brought together perfectly.

The Potential and the Actual

The problem with this change of view is that the arguments that Aristotle had used previously against the primacy of universals, or Platonic "forms", work just as well against the primacy of species. In Books Theta and Eta, he takes yet another position. Here he argues that the important distinction in metaphysics is between the **potential** and the **actual**. In the world, we only find things that have been actualized.

ALL SUBSTANCES CONSIST OF BOTH ACTUALITY AND POTENTIALITY, OF FORM AND MATTER.

*THE FIRST IS THAT WHICH **DETERMINES**, THE SECOND THAT WHICH IS **DETERMINED**.*

TOTAL ACTUAL

TOTAL POTENTIAL

72 Thus we can see a continuum of existence.

At its lowest and most imperfect, existence is all matter, a chaotic and characterless pool of potentiality. At its highest it is the Supreme Being, or Supreme Cause, which is perfect, contains no potentiality, no matter, and is therefore fully actual.

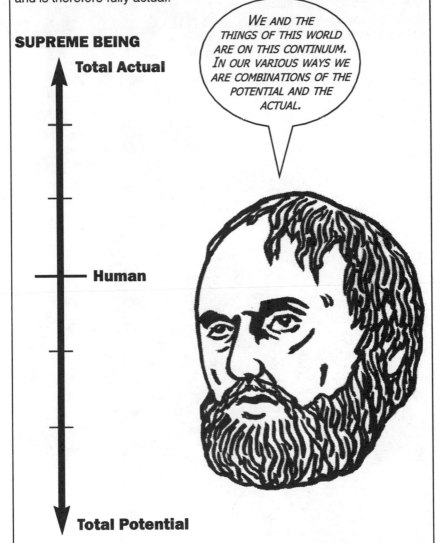

SUPREME BEING

Total Actual

WE AND THE THINGS OF THIS WORLD ARE ON THIS CONTINUUM. IN OUR VARIOUS WAYS WE ARE COMBINATIONS OF THE POTENTIAL AND THE ACTUAL.

Human

Total Potential

Here we have Aristotle's principle of being. In this way, Aristotle believed that he had achieved the first of the two aims of his metaphysical studies. He had described a world of things that largely correspond with our common-sense experience of them. The second aim is to work out how we can have scientific knowledge of that world.

What is Logic?

In *The Metaphysics*, Aristotle describes what, at the most basic level, we can know. He also needed to explain how we can know it, which he does largely in *The Organon*. The Greek word for language, as well as for "reason" was *logos*, which is the root of our word, logic. He saw humans as essentially rational creatures.

RATIONALITY IS A PART OF THE NATURE OF WHAT IT IS TO BE HUMAN.

SO THE FACT THAT WE HUMANS USE LANGUAGE MEANS THAT WE ARE RATIONAL AND, INDEED, LOGICAL.

As we have seen, this is not to say that we are always rational or that we never make mistakes. But it does mean that we can be rational, and, in his work on logic, he was trying to systematize language, to make it work more logically and therefore more effectively.

Logic and Doing Science

Aristotle wanted to establish logic as a way of doing science, a way of **knowing** things. All of our knowledge must be rooted in sense experiences of the things of this world, the substances. He says that there is "nothing in our intellect that was not first in the senses". However, because we are rational, we can go beyond this knowledge of things. We can detect in substances their essences. We can discover the intelligible, **non-material** qualities of things.

WE HAVE AN ABILITY TO ABSTRACT, TO DRAW CONCLUSIONS AND TO GENERALIZE.

THIS NEW KNOWLEDGE OF THE INTELLIGIBLE IS **SCIENCE.**

And although science is dependent on sense experience, it is also superior to sense experience. To use his terms from *The Metaphysics*, sense experience is **potentially intelligible** while proper scientific knowledge is **actually intelligible**.

A Satisfying Conclusion

The universals (such as species and genus) that science deals with are non-material things that are present in particular objects. They are hidden by the individual characteristics of the objects. We humans can reach through this veil of appearances to see the real essences within. There is a satisfying way for him to conclude this account of knowledge that would solve the ontological questions raised by the metaphysics.

ARE THE UNIVERSALS REAL THINGS IN THE WORLD, OR ARE THEY MENTAL, LINGUISTIC DEVICES?

He could say that the universals "dog" and "animal" are really in this particular dog, but are only fully actual when they are in the mind, as part of our understanding of the doggy world in general.

Deductive Interference

The key task of science was to establish definitions, and Aristotle thought this could only be done in a limited number of ways. His basic logical term was the **syllogism**. In this, he was establishing key principles of **deductive inference**. When we infer something deductively, we are gaining a new piece of knowledge by mentally working it out from other pieces of knowledge, rather than through sense experience. The conclusion, the new knowledge, follows necessarily from the old knowledge.

PYTHAGORAS' THEOREM IS A GOOD EXAMPLE OF THIS.

HERE WE BEGIN WITH SOMETHING SELF-EVIDENTLY TRUE. WE CAN SEE QUITE PLAINLY THE NATURE OF A RIGHT-ANGLE TRIANGLE.

EUCLID

The Truth of Pythagoras' Theorem

Pythagoras' theorem concludes that "the square on the hypotenuse is equal to the sum of the squares on the opposite two sides". But this is not at all self-evident. How do we know it is true?

For it not to be true would involve a **contradiction** which effectively says that something **is** and **is not** at the same time.

The Syllogism or Valid Deduction

The syllogisms that Aristotle worked with are much simpler than Pythagoras' Theorem. He thought that there were four "perfect" syllogisms of deduction. All arguments that were deductively valid could be expressed in them, perhaps after some simplification. Each has two premises and a conclusion. The best known syllogism, which tends to crop up often in logic textbooks is …

Premise 1: All men are mortal.
Premise 2: Socrates is a man.
Conclusion: Therefore, Socrates is mortal.

WE CAN SEE HOW THIS MIGHT WORK IN SCIENCE BY TAKING AN EXAMPLE FROM THE NATURAL WORLD …

All broad-leaved trees are deciduous.
Vines are broad-leaved.
Therefore, vines are deciduous.

Higher-level Syllogisms

In this second syllogism, Aristotle considers that he is explaining, or "demonstrating", to use his term, the nature of vines in a logical and rational way. As we have seen in his metaphysics, he believed that there is a hierarchy of being, starting with individual substances and rising level by level into more general and universal classifications and explanations. In this case he asks why deciduous trees are deciduous. He decides that it is because in them the sap coagulates at the base of the leaf.

THEREFORE, "DECIDUOUS" MEANS "SAP-COAGULATOR", AND WE HAVE A NEW SYLLOGISM AT A HIGHER LEVEL.

All sap-coagulators are deciduous.
All broad-leaved trees are sap-coagulators.
Therefore, all broad-leaved trees are deciduous.

Rules of Thought

Aristotle's logic wants to show two things: first, that levels of being are linked by **necessity** – there is a guarantee of no alternative to the conclusion drawn; second, that our rational nature can **recognize** this necessity.

TO ACHIEVE THIS GUARANTEED NECESSITY WE MUST ABIDE BY CERTAIN KEY PRINCIPLES OF THINKING OR "RULES OF THOUGHT".

He saw two as being particularly important. The Principle of Non-Contradiction states that of two contradictory statements, for example, "it is raining" and "it is not raining", only one of them can be true, the other must be false. The Principle of Excluded Middle says that at least one of them is true.

The Two Principles

The first principle says that it cannot be raining and not raining at the same time – "not both". The second principle says that it must be either raining or not raining – "not neither". If we deny these principles, then everything that we say, all claims that we make about the world, will be the same and will be meaningless.

Aristotle also recognized that if we deny these principles, then we have no means of making judgements about how people should behave.

IF I SAY THAT MURDER IS NEITHER RIGHT NOR WRONG, THEN I ABOLISH THE CONCEPT OF MURDER, AND PEOPLE CAN DO WHAT THEY LIKE.

These are not rules of **language**, because we clearly can say these sorts of things. Neither are they rules describing how the **world** works. They are about how **thinking** works.

Induction

Deduction is not the only kind of argument that Aristotle identifies. He does also discuss **inductive** argument, where we infer a general claim from observations of a number of particular examples. If I see a hundred swans and they are all white, I might then feel able to say "all swans are white".

THIS, OF COURSE, DOES NOT HAVE TO BE TRUE. IT IS NOT TRUE OF **NECESSITY**.

The moment I see a black swan, I will know that it is false. Therefore inductive arguments are distinctly different from deductive arguments. We could only make it necessarily true that all swans are white if I had seen every swan that ever has been or will be.

In general, inductive arguments are useful in allowing us to draw tentative conclusions about things we have not experienced on the basis of things that we have experienced, but their reliability is always questionable. For example, we might note that every broad-leaved tree that we have come across has been deciduous. We might conclude on the basis of this that **all** broad-leaved trees are deciduous. We might be wrong. There might be a broad-leaved tree that isn't deciduous. But for the time being it is a useful piece of information.

The Dialectic

Induction and deduction can be seen together as demonstration. Aristotle also describes another method of argument, the **dialectic**, in *The Topics*. This was a method of contest developed before Aristotle. Zeno and other pre-Socratics introduced it. Socrates, in Plato's dialogues, used it devastatingly on his opponents.

TWO PEOPLE TAKE DIFFERENT POSITIONS, AND, AS IN CHESS, ATTACK AND DEFEND ...

QUESTIONS ARE PURSUED TO EXPOSE CONTRADICTIONS, UNTIL THE OPPONENT'S VIEW IS REDUCED TO AGREEMENT.

Such a method might seem a clever sport, and it could be used like this by Sophists to show off their skills. But it has a serious purpose.

The Agon

Two things were especially important to the Greeks. The spoken word in rivalry to arrive at **consensus** was a basis of city-state democracy. Rivalry between states was also ritualized in the athletic festivals held at Olympia. From the word *agon* – "contest" – came *antagonism* – "opposed in contest".

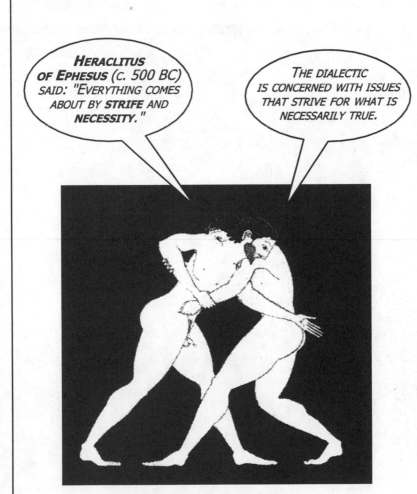

HERACLITUS OF EPHESUS (c. 500 BC) SAID: "EVERYTHING COMES ABOUT BY STRIFE AND NECESSITY."

THE DIALECTIC IS CONCERNED WITH ISSUES THAT STRIVE FOR WHAT IS NECESSARILY TRUE.

G.W.F. Hegel (1770-1831) would later make dialectics a process of reality itself. But, for Aristotle, it was inferior to logic which establishes truth by proofs.

Primary Propositions

Using observations of the world and treating them deductively and inductively, we can trace our way up the hierarchy of scientific knowledge. This will reveal to us the causes of what is necessarily true (or so Aristotle thought). However, what is at the top of the hierarchy? Here Aristotle becomes rather mysterious. He says that there will be a few starting points or first principles from which everything else flows.

THESE ARE THE PRIMARY PROPOSITIONS WHICH BEGAN AND WHICH DRIVE THE COSMOS. THEY CANNOT BE KNOWN IN THE NORMAL WAY.

If he is right in his picture of a deductively logical universe, then each proposition is derived from the one above. We follow the trail upwards.

The Problem of *"Nous"*

But the propositions at the very top have nothing above them and so cannot be explained. Aristotle is quite happy with this. Scientific knowledge is knowledge of causes …

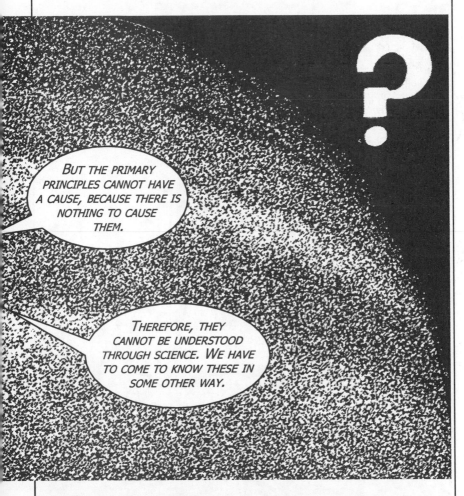

Aristotle called this ability to make progressive jumps up to first principles *nous*, "mind", "a thought", "purpose" or "resolve". But there is no general agreement on what Aristotle thought this was. Some say that it is a kind of intuition that allows us to recognize these first principles as self-evident. However, this seems to contradict the empirical nature of so much of his work.

The Great Chain of Being

Aristotle's idea of a hierarchy of knowledge became very influential among Christian theologians in the Middle Ages. It was transformed by them into knowledge of a divinely ordained hierarchy. **Thomas Aquinas** (c. 1225-74), the leading Aristotelian theologian, in his *Summa theologiae*, describes a "Hierarchy of Being" in the Universe.

A GREAT CHAIN OF BEING STRETCHES DOWN FROM GOD, THROUGH ANGELS AND THEN HUMANS, ANIMALS, PLANTS AND ALL MATERIAL ELEMENTS.

The links between the material and spiritual are real and necessary for the full expression of God's divine goodness and purpose. The human intellect is drawn up this hierarchy, link by link, to fulfil its ultimate purpose, which is the contemplation of God himself.

Dante's *Divine Comedy* (c. 1307) dramatized this route from the infernal regions to paradise in the quest for divine contemplation. The architecture of his great theological epic draws on Aristotle, Aquinas and, some say, Islamic influences.

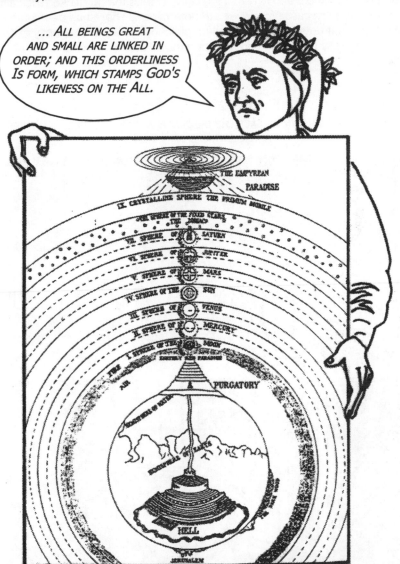

... ALL BEINGS GREAT AND SMALL ARE LINKED IN ORDER; AND THIS ORDERLINESS IS FORM, WHICH STAMPS GOD'S LIKENESS ON THE ALL.

Theological ecologists today also insist on reverence for the hierarchical order and design of nature. Bio-diversity is a divine ordination. The careless elimination of whole species of plants and animals is actually sinful, because God is in all of them.

Determinism

Aristotle's methodology seems to give us a very deterministic picture of the world. When we have done the explanatory work, we will see that everything in the world is linked logically. Things that are linked logically are linked by necessity, so they are determined. There has been much discussion of determinism in modern philosophy. So what exactly Aristotle really meant has great importance. He did not write much about determinism as such.

IN ONE WELL-KNOWN PASSAGE, HE DESCRIBES A MAN WHO BECOMES THIRSTY AFTER EATING SPICY FOOD ...

HE GOES OUT TO GET A DRINK, IS MUGGED AND DIES.

WE COULD SAY THAT THE MAN'S LIKING FOR SPICY FOOD DETERMINED HIS DEATH. THIS WOULD IN A SENSE BE TRUE.

HOWEVER, IF SOMEONE ASKED **WHY** HE DIED, THE ANSWER "BECAUSE HE LIKED CURRY" WOULD HARDLY BE ENOUGH.

It would not be an **explanation** of his death. Maybe we need to distinguish between deterministic causality and explanation in its normal sense. Aristotle was interested in general patterns that are largely invariable, not individual events.

How "Empirical" was Aristotle?

How does Aristotle's scientific methodology measure up to modern science? Not very well, despite the fact that for two millennia almost everyone believed almost everything that he said. He was far more empirical than any other of the ancients, but not empirical enough. He had a methodology of science, but lacked an **experimental** methodology by which explanations and theories could be shown to be valid or false. In *Parts of Animals*, he says ...

CONCERNING PERISHABLE THINGS - PLANTS AND ANIMALS - WE ARE MUCH BETTER PLACED, SINCE WE LIVE AMONG THEM; AND ANYONE WHO WANTS TO TAKE SUFFICIENT TROUBLE MAY GRASP MANY THINGS ABOUT EVERY KIND THAT EXIST.

This is admirably scientific in its sentiment, but in practice he did not recognize the need to test theory directly against empirical observation.

The *Historia Animalium*, for example, contains a mass of information on animals but it seems to us to be disorganized and anecdotal – and in part fantasy. He is occasionally rigorous, as when he says …

THE VELOCITY OF AN OBJECT MOVING AT ITS NATURAL SPEED IS PROPORTIONAL TO ITS SIZE AND INVERSELY PROPORTIONAL TO THE RESISTANCE OF WHATEVER IT IS MOVING THROUGH.

THIS SEEMS LIKE A MODERN EQUATION AND WOULD HAVE BEEN TESTABLE.

BUT THIS KIND OF RIGOUR AND TESTABILITY TENDED TO BE EXCEPTIONAL IN ARISTOTLE'S WORK.

Assumptions and Misconceptions

Another problem arose from the way that Aristotle made assumptions. These were probably common sense in Athens at the time but were unwarranted. For example, he assumes that right is better than left, upper better than lower and front better than back, and tries to apply this principle to the universe. Thus, the "sublunary" world below the moon is naturally inferior to the world above and beyond the moon. He also considered the possibility that there were animals on the moon that lived in fire.

BECAUSE, HERE ON EARTH, THERE ARE ANIMALS THAT LIVE IN THE OTHER THREE ELEMENTS OF MATTER – EARTH, AIR AND WATER.

... SO, BY LOGICAL INDUCTIONS IT MIGHT BE THAT ANIMALS ON THE MOON CAN LIVE ON THE FOURTH ELEMENT – FIRE.

He assumed without question that men were superior in all respects to women, and used this assumption to form a basis for his theory of reproduction.

MEN HAVE THE ABILITY TO COMPOSE THE BLOOD INTO SOMETHING THAT WILL BE THE FORM FOR A NEW HUMAN.

WOMEN PROVIDED ONLY THE **MATTER.**

Aristotle's Science

Finally, it may be that any scientific methodology that tries to combine causally determined explanations with teleological explanations must remain confused. We can divide Aristotle's work on science into physics, cosmology, meteorology, biology and psychology. But often this distinction fails to work.

In any case, "knowledge" as such was just beginning. There is no reason why we should assume that he would include the same topics within his broad subject headings as has become the convention today.

Position and Motion

Zeno believed that whatever knowledge we had of the world was illusory, and used his paradoxes to support his argument. The paradoxes seem to demonstrate that time and motion cannot exist. They were a major challenge to Aristotle. To counter them, Aristotle had to demonstrate that space was infinitely divisible.

THIS DOES NOT MEAN THAT THERE ARE AN INFINITE NUMBER OF *THINGS*.

THE UNIVERSE IS FINITE. IT DOES NOT EXTEND ENDLESSLY AND DOES NOT CONTAIN AN INFINITE AMOUNT OF MATTER, AS THE ATOMISTS BELIEVE.

A Theory of the Universe

The universe is finite because the things that it contains have a "natural" motion and place in relation to each other. This would be impossible if there were no "natural" boundaries. Things have qualities of lightness and heaviness (which Aristotle thought were equivalent concepts – lightness was not an absence of heaviness) and these qualities determine the natural position of the thing.

The motions of things will be simple and many would have a natural end. The natural end would be the natural place for the thing to be. Above the moon is a realm of perfection where things have a permanent circular motion. This motion is eternal so it never stops, but the circles the things describe are themselves finite.

This is a sophisticated theory, and it's not surprising that it was believed for so long – for nearly two thousand years. The evidence for it is clear. Heavy things do always fall downwards.

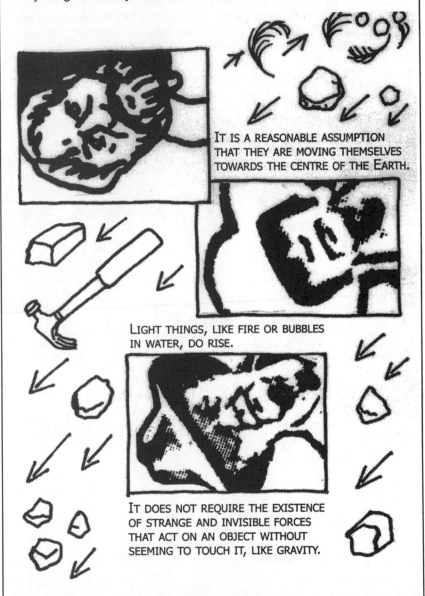

IT IS A REASONABLE ASSUMPTION THAT THEY ARE MOVING THEMSELVES TOWARDS THE CENTRE OF THE EARTH.

LIGHT THINGS, LIKE FIRE OR BUBBLES IN WATER, DO RISE.

IT DOES NOT REQUIRE THE EXISTENCE OF STRANGE AND INVISIBLE FORCES THAT ACT ON AN OBJECT WITHOUT SEEMING TO TOUCH IT, LIKE GRAVITY.

This is exactly in line with the project of his lifetime. It is a simple theory with simple processes which explains a wide variety of phenomena, and which is in accordance with common sense.

Incorrect Dynamics

Aristotle's ideas on dynamics were similarly at once scientific, in accordance with common sense, and wrong. The speed at which an object travels is proportionate to its weight. The heavier it is, the faster it goes. Drop two balls, one half the weight of the other, from a high place and the heavier ball will reach the ground in half the time of the lighter one.

Not until nearly two thousand years later did Galileo try this out, and find that it wasn't true.

The Cosmos

Aristotle saw the universe as a series of concentric spheres. Those on the outside contained the heavenly bodies, which were made of "ether", an element alongside earth, air, fire and water but one that could not be changed or destroyed.

BELOW THE MOON THERE IS NO ETHER, AND SO THE ELEMENTS ARE LIABLE TO DECAY AND TRANSFORMATION.

THE ATMOSPHERE CONSISTS OF TWO LAYERS: AN INNER SPHERE OF AIR AND AN OUTER SPHERE WHICH IS NOT ACTUALLY FIRE BUT WHICH IS VERY INFLAMMABLE.

ARISTOTLE SAYS THAT THE HEAT THAT WE KNOW COMES FROM THE SUN ACTUALLY COMES FROM THIS FIRE SPHERE AS THE SUN PUSHES THROUGH IT.

An Odd Mixture

Aristotle deals with many of these cosmic matters in *Meteorology*, along with the Aurora Borealis, comets, the Milky Way, rain, clouds, dew and hoar frost, snow, hail, winds, rivers, springs, climate, coastal change, where does the sea come from and why is it salty, more on winds, earthquakes, volcanoes, thunder and lightning, hurricanes, haloes and rainbows.

Most of his ideas and explanations are quite wrong and some seem to have few roots in observation at all. Sometimes, though, he gets it almost right. His explanation of the sea is a case in point.

Then he spoils it by saying that the salt is a kind of residue that falls from the clouds in rain, and that he himself has observed that the sea is therefore becoming more and more salty. We need to remember that Aristotle was a product of the ancient world. The dominant cultural force of his day was mythology. Aristotle's science was new and radical. It would have been impossible for it to be perfect. He made many mistakes, and his major fault – interpreting observations in a way that supported his theories – was a major handicap.

Psychology

The Greek word for soul is *"psyche"* (or *"psuche"*), from which comes our word "psychology". It would be a mistake to understand the word "soul" in a modern sense. Aristotle saw it as meaning the essence or life force within all living things – that which made them grow and gave them their shape. Soul is pure form, the body is matter.

*MY PSYCHOLOGY IS ABOUT THE DISTINCTION BETWEEN THE **LIVING** AND THE **NON-LIVING**, NOT BETWEEN THE MIND AND THE BODY.*

IT IS IN SOME WAYS AS MUCH A STUDY OF PLANTS AND ANIMALS AS IT IS OF THE HUMAN MIND.

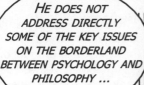

HE DOES NOT ADDRESS DIRECTLY SOME OF THE KEY ISSUES ON THE BORDERLAND BETWEEN PSYCHOLOGY AND PHILOSOPHY ...

SUCH AS THE QUESTION OF CONSCIOUSNESS AND WHETHER IT IS A MATERIAL OR A NON-MATERIAL PHENOMENON.

Neither does he discuss directly the issue of free will versus determinism (are we humans choosing freely when we act and make decisions, or are we biological robots, machines driven to act according to physical and environmental drives and constraints?). Nevertheless, we can work out from what he does say what his likely responses to these questions might be.

Consciousness: a Product of History

We think of questions of consciousness and freedom as central and we imagine them to have always been so. But they may be a product of our cultural and intellectual history over the last few hundred years. The social and political transformations of the 18th-century Enlightenment, from which sprang our political institutions and culture, also necessarily produced a new conception of what it is to be human. This was a picture of humanity which highlighted the individual as a free and conscious being.

BECAUSE WITHOUT THAT CONSCIOUS FREEDOM, HUMANS CANNOT FULFIL THEIR ROLES WITHIN THE NEW AND EMERGING POLITICAL INSTITUTIONS.

DEMOCRACY NEEDS FREELY CHOSEN ACTION.

AND SUCH ACTION NEEDS SELF-AWARENESS.

Aristotle and the other ancients solved these problems in other ways.

Mind and Body

As we might expect from someone who emphasizes observation and sees the explanation of physically existing things as the task of science, Aristotle's psychology is an extension of his physical science, and his explanations are in physical terms. For Aristotle, the psyche was the "principle" of the body, that which allowed the body the power of self-movement and of self-directed growth. In the end, the picture he gives is at the same time deterministic and voluntary.

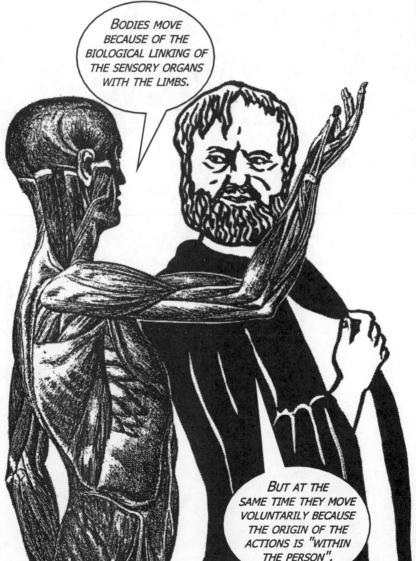

The Capacities of the Soul

In a predictably teleological manner, he approaches the psyche in terms of its capacities. The soul is what it can do. In the same way, the sense organs of the body are essentially what they can do. He uses the eye as an example. Sight is the "soul" of the eye. The soul of a human is the sum of a human's capacities.

We have, in common with both plants and animals, a "nutritive" capacity.

THIS IS THE ABILITY TO GROW, TO THRIVE AND TO CARRY OUT BASIC BIOLOGICAL FUNCTIONS.

THIS IS QUITE UNCONNECTED TO ANY OF THE HIGHER FUNCTIONS OF HUMANS, BUT IS, NEVERTHELESS, VITAL TO THEIR WELL-BEING.

We also share with animals a capacity for sensation and movement – and these two are inextricably linked.

He recognizes the five sense organs, and believes that their particular capacity is to abstract from the things in the world their form, while leaving the matter behind.

The picture Aristotle gives us of this process is of a ring or seal of metal being pressed into soft wax and leaving its impression. The things in the world impress themselves on our senses.

The Brain

One might ask where the brain fits in. The answer is one that we now find impossible to accept. It does not. Aristotle thought of the brain as a fairly useless, grey, cold lump.

IT MIGHT CONCEIVABLY BE FOR COOLING BLOOD THAT HAD BECOME OVERHEATED.

The key organ for him was the heart. He saw this as the master sense-organ to which all the other sense-organs sent their messages – a sort of mental clearing house and sorting office. It was here that perception, memory and motivation took place. Interestingly, when the Egyptians mummified the body for reincarnation, they too had no use for the brain: it was thrown away but the heart was preserved.

The Objects of Sensation

The particular objects of the senses can be of three kinds. First, there is that which is particular to each sense.

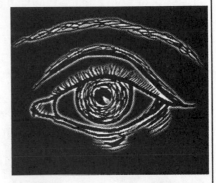

SUCH AS COLOUR FOR THE EYE
OR SOUND FOR THE EARS.

Second, those objects that are jointly grasped by some or all of the senses together.

SUCH AS MOVEMENT OR SHAPE.

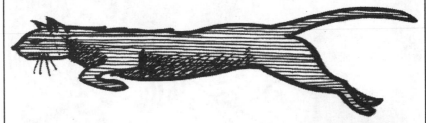

Third, our senses may grasp a particular sensation and then infer some particular knowledge from it.

FOR EXAMPLE, WE MAY HEAR A VOICE
IN THE DARK AND RECOGNIZE IT AS
THE VOICE OF A FRIEND.

In the last case, we are acting on **imagination**. And where does that come from?

Imagination and Memory

Imagination is the "movement which results upon an actual sensation". It is the holding up of the image of sensation before the heart (or mind, as we would say), and the retention of the image is, of course, memory.

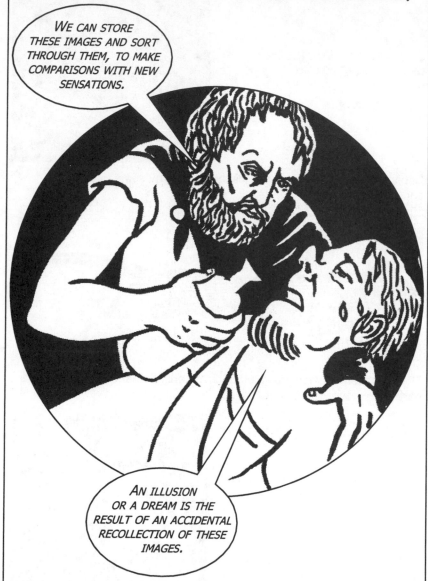

WE CAN STORE THESE IMAGES AND SORT THROUGH THEM, TO MAKE COMPARISONS WITH NEW SENSATIONS.

AN ILLUSION OR A DREAM IS THE RESULT OF AN ACCIDENTAL RECOLLECTION OF THESE IMAGES.

In a fever, for example, the disruption to the heart from the illness may throw up a disordered and meaningless collection of images.

Transformation into Universals

These things we have in common with animals. What then is it that distinguishes us from animals? It is of course reason, and in Aristotle's writings the capacity for reason seems like another, "seventh", sense organ. The ordinary senses deal with the concrete and the particular.

THEY DETACH THE FORM FROM THE SUBSTANCE, BUT IDENTIFY IT ONLY AS ONE PARTICULAR FORM — THAT **ONE**, OVER **THERE**.

REASON ALLOWS HUMANS TO ABSTRACT FORM AND TO TRANSFORM IT INTO UNIVERSALS.

Reason provides and constructs a context for individual sensations. It is a kind of intuitive ability and is rather mysterious.

Active and Passive Reason

There have been countless interpretations of the difficult passage of *De Anima* which deals with this mysterious and "intuitive ability". There is no general agreement on what he meant. But it seems a likely interpretation to say that there is both an **active** and a **passive** reason.

It builds on the sorted and organized objects of sensation to create the kind of hierarchy of reason which Aristotle seems to have believed could reach up to the supreme being, to pure reason contemplating itself.

Here Aristotle seems to become almost religious. He has been interpreted as meaning that there is something of the divine in all of us, and that while individual self-awareness is finite, the active reason within us is not, it is immortal. He is not alone in this kind of sentiment. **Bertrand Russell** (1872-1970) concludes his book *The Problems of Philosophy* with this thought …

THROUGH THE GREATNESS OF THE UNIVERSE WHICH PHILOSOPHY CONTEMPLATES, THE MIND ALSO IS RENDERED GREAT, AND BECOMES CAPABLE OF THAT UNION WITH THE UNIVERSE WHICH CONSTITUTES ITS HIGHEST GOOD.

The Ethics

Aristotle's ethics are found in two treatises, the *Nicomachean Ethics* and the *Eudemian Ethics*. As usual, the text is confusing and contains many digressions, but a consistent and coherent ethical theory lies within. Virtue ethics, sometimes called *"aretaic"* ethics from the Greek word for virtue, forms one of the three major ethical theories that dominate moral philosophy. The other two are *consequentialism* and *deontology*.

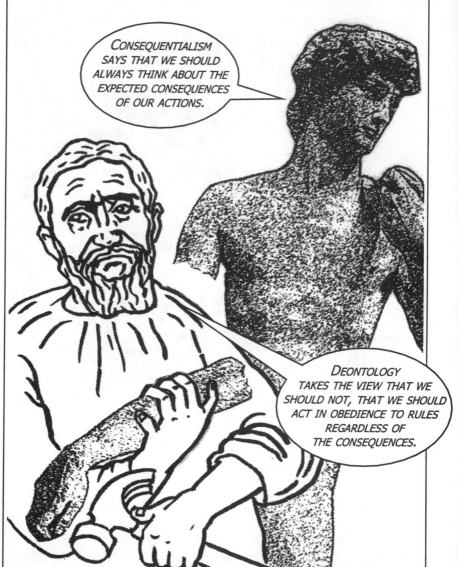

CONSEQUENTIALISM SAYS THAT WE SHOULD ALWAYS THINK ABOUT THE EXPECTED CONSEQUENCES OF OUR ACTIONS.

DEONTOLOGY TAKES THE VIEW THAT WE SHOULD NOT, THAT WE SHOULD ACT IN OBEDIENCE TO RULES REGARDLESS OF THE CONSEQUENCES.

A Flourishing Life

Aristotle's lectures on ethics were intended for young men and were a response to the question "What should I do to live a flourishing life?". This is not a question about what they should do to ensure that their life contained the signs of success, such as money, power or public regard. These might be necessary for the successful life, but they don't constitute it.

THE QUESTION IS RATHER ABOUT HOW TO ENJOY LIFE AND GET THE MOST FROM IT.

The answer, which follows from his teleological metaphysics, is that this will happen if they live their lives fully in accordance with the **purpose** or **function** of a human being. To do this, they must live both rationally and virtuously, which makes Aristotle's writings on these topics a work of moral philosophy rather than the kind of self-help book found in railway station bookstores.

Eudaimonia

This "life-plan" all sounds rather stilted and unnatural when it is translated into English. A "contented, fulfilled and flourishing life with added serenity and lots of activity" about sums it up.

The Greeks, however, had one word, *"eudaimonia"*, to describe this kind of desirable life. *Eudaimonia* derives in Greek from *eu* (well, good or right) *daimon* (the "demon" or indwelling spirit). How to achieve it was a major topic for debate.

Could it be fame and public recognition? Aristotle does think that it is important to be well respected by others and to have self-respect, but these cannot be final ends. In any case, as he perceptively points out ...

It could also be a life of pleasure, but he has firm views about this. He sees pleasure as **a** good but not **the** Good.

Is Pleasure a Good?

Aristotle points out that powerful men often seem to dedicate their lives to pleasure, perhaps simply because they can. This sets a bad example, and many others try to emulate them. But this is to live a life suited only to animals and children.

For him, pleasure is something that **perfects** an activity. When we are wrapped up in some useful and productive work we lose ourselves in it, especially if we are doing it well. We cease to notice the passing of time.

This, for Aristotle, is real pleasure.

Contemplation Is Happiness

In fact, he believes that "perfect" happiness can only be found in intellectual contemplation. A life spent in the investigation and admiration of the natural universe is the very best activity for humans. Wisdom (the Greek word is *"sophia"*, hence *philo* (love) *sophia* or "philosophy" – love of wisdom) is the supreme intellectual virtue, a combination of scientific knowledge and intuition.

THE SUPREME BEING CONSISTS ENTIRELY OF REASON AND SPENDS ETERNITY CONTEMPLATING ITSELF.

THE SUPREME BEING IS THE UNMOVED MOVER, THAT WHICH CHANGES OTHERS BUT IS NOT ITSELF SUBJECT TO CHANGE.

WE HUMANS HAVE A SPARK OF THE SUPREME BEING IN US, OUR RATIONALITY.

THEREFORE, WHEN WE CONTEMPLATE THE UNCHANGING UNIVERSE WE ARE BEING ABOUT AS DIVINE AS WE HUMANS CAN BE.

This kind of contemplation is like a form of prayer. "If the intellect is divine compared with man, the life of the intellect must be divine compared with the life of a human being." Again, "we ought, so far as in us lies, to put on immortality, and do all that we can to live in conformity with the highest that is in us."

The Influence of Emotions on Reason

Since it is obvious to us and to Aristotle that only a tiny minority of people will be able to spend a lifetime in contemplation – those rich enough, for one thing – it remains something of a curiosity. However, he had other things to say about *eudaimonia*, which gave his Ethics their power and lasting significance.

The soul consists of a rational and an irrational part. A major element of the irrational part of the soul is our emotions – such as love, fear, pity and joy. These emotions have a powerful influence on our actions and often can lead us into trouble. Therefore, we need to be able to control our emotions.

IF WE CAN FEEL THE RIGHT EMOTIONS AT THE RIGHT TIME AND IN THE RIGHT DEGREE, THEN WE WILL TEND TO ACT WELL AND CONSISTENTLY AND WILL LEAD A SUCCESSFUL LIFE.

However, emotions are difficult to control. It is usually impossible to stop feeling an emotion, even if we know that it is inappropriate or damaging.

The Virtue of the Soul

Aristotle's advice is that we should align our emotions with what is the right thing to do in particular circumstances, so that we **want** to do what is **right**. And "right" here means that which is rational. If a man is faced with great temptation to do something wicked – to steal, perhaps – and gives in, then he is unlikely to be happy and contented in the long run.

HE MAY WELL BE CAUGHT.

HE WILL GAIN A REPUTATION FOR DISHONESTY AND PEOPLE WILL NOT TRUST HIM.

The police will keep checking on him and he will need to worry about concealing his dishonesty.

On the other hand, if he resists the temptation but only with great difficulty he is still not likely to have much peace of mind. Life as a constant battle with temptation is not much fun.

ONLY IF HE IS NOT EVEN TEMPTED IN THE FIRST PLACE, OR IF HE IS ABLE TO DISMISS THE TEMPTATION EASILY, WILL HE BE CONTENTED AND HAPPY.

We might **admire** someone who overcomes great temptation, but we would rather be the person who is not tempted at all. It is this last state that Aristotle recommends for humans. It is "virtuous activity of the soul". **127**

The Doctrine of the Mean

Aristotle thought that the only realistic way to control emotions is to train them by practice and habit, to habituate oneself into feeling emotions appropriately. Moral argument does not work. Aristotle doesn't mean that we should train ourselves not to have emotions at all. They are a normal and natural part of being human. This training consists of the development of what he calls moral virtues. "Virtue" has a kind of old-fashioned feel to it and is often described as an excellence of character.

IT IS POSSIBLY BEST THOUGHT OF AS A SETTLED WAY OF FEELING EMOTIONS, SO THAT IN ANY GIVEN SITUATION WE BOTH FEEL THE RIGHT EMOTION AND WE FEEL IT IN THE RIGHT DEGREE.

WE SHOULD THEN DO THE RIGHT THING.

Feeling an emotion either too strongly or too weakly are both wrong.
They are vices. For example, courage is the moral virtue that we need to
deal with the emotion of fear. However, we don't want to eliminate fear,
since it is often a useful and even vital means of survival. The trick is to
feel it in the right intensity.

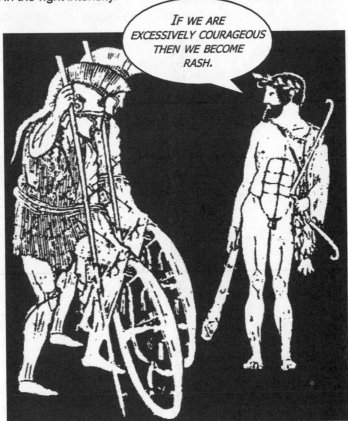

*IF WE ARE
EXCESSIVELY COURAGEOUS
THEN WE BECOME
RASH.*

*IF WE ARE NOT
COURAGEOUS ENOUGH, WE
FEEL FEAR TOO MUCH AND
BECOME COWARDLY.*

Rashness and cowardice are both vices.
If we are prone to either of them we will
be unable to lead a settled, contented life.
This is Aristotle's famous Doctrine of the
Mean – the "middle way" or
"nothing to excess".

Generosity and the Average

Each virtue is a "mean", or average, set between two vices – one of excess and one of deficiency. Generosity is an important virtue that bonds us to each other. Life would be the bleaker without it. It is obviously possible to be insufficiently generous. Such a person would have the vice of meanness. But it is also possible to be excessively generous.

Someone who is well-off should give more than someone who is poor. Also, some people are more deserving of generosity than others. It follows with a brutal sort of practicality that a strong, fit young man **should** be braver than an older man who is past his prime.

The Role of the State

The training that all of this virtue requires is difficult, but not impossible. Young people have to start early, and they need the guidance of their elders, their family and of the state. The state has a particular responsibility for habituating people into virtues because it can pass laws.

For example, by forcing themselves to be generous to others, and by accepting guidance from older people about who to be generous to, and how generous to be, the young will, eventually, turn themselves into generous people. Adolescent rebellion does not seem to be a factor that Aristotle considers in his Ethics.

Good Advice

This is the basis for Aristotle's moral map. To be happy we need to be virtuous, we need to be people of excellent character. We achieve this by training and habituating ourselves into particular dispositions towards emotions which are mid-way between excess and deficiency. But is this enough? How can we be **sure** that we are doing the right thing? Aristotle has some practical advice. Of the two vices, the excess and the deficiency of a virtue, one is generally worse than the other.

IN THIS WAY, COWARDICE IS WORSE THAN RASHNESS. WE SHOULD BE PARTICULARLY WARY OF THIS VICE.

We must be candid with ourselves about our own failings and bad habits, and "drag ourselves in the contrary direction". Lastly, be wary of pleasure, because it clouds our judgement. Develop and use the virtue of practical wisdom or prudence. This is the practical, rough and ready skill of judgement and decision-making. It helps us to work out what is best for ourselves in both the long and short term.

All this moderate common sense might sound rather boring but is vital for the virtuous and therefore happy life. Intellectuals can often be very bad at the practical aspects of everyday life.

Without practical wisdom we can attain to none of the other intellectual or moral virtues. It is a prerequisite for virtuous living and good citizenship.

Virtue Ethics Today

A number of modern philosophers think that virtue theory, as it is now called, is really the best way to think about ethics.

Other philosophers, feminists in particular, deny that ethics can be forced into "systems" such as consequentialism or deontology.

The Politics

Aristotle was not politically correct. Slaves and women had no role in the political community. Slaves did not posses the rationality that was needed for an active and positive role, and women, although they had the rationality, did not have the authority. He was not alone in these views – indeed, to have thought anything else in his day would have amounted to heresy.

HIS ARGUMENTS FOR SLAVERY AND THE SUBJUGATION OF WOMEN ARE NOT VERY CONVINCING.

HOWEVER, OTHER THAN THIS, HIS POLITICAL VIEWS WERE BENEVOLENT AND PROGRESSIVE.

MAINSTREAM DEMOCRATIC POLITICIANS TODAY OWE MUCH TO HIS LEGACY.

Communitarian principles of mutual responsibility and regard between the people and the state can be traced back eventually to Aristotle's work.

Politics and Ethics

Aristotle's politics are rooted in his ethics. They are aspects of the same question. How can humans live such as to be their best? How can they fulfil themselves?

THE QUESTION NORMALLY ASKED TODAY IS ALMOST THE CONVERSE. HOW SHOULD PEOPLE ACT SO AS TO MEET THEIR OBLIGATIONS TO THEIR COMMUNITY?

PEOPLE ARE **ESSENTIALLY** SOCIAL AND CAN ONLY BE PROPERLY HUMAN **IN** A COMMUNITY ...

TO LIVE VIRTUOUSLY AND RATIONALLY CAN ONLY MEAN TO LIVE WELL WITH OTHER PEOPLE.

We have an unavoidable obligation to take part in community life and bear responsibility for its decisions. But the community has no life of its own. It is there to fulfil each individual's purpose, not its own ends. There is no hint of totalitarianism in Aristotle's work. The limit of the state's power is that beyond which it ceases to serve its citizens.

The Family as Political Economy

The cornerstone of Aristotle's politics is the classical Greek city state or *polis*. We get our word "politics" from that and the term for free citizen *polites*. Another commonly used word is "economy", which derives from the Greek *oikonomia*, meaning *oikos* (household) and *nomos* (law, usage, manage). Our long tradition of "political economy" was originally a matter of "citizens' family business". And this was a fundamental unit of social life in Greece.

This was generally believed by Greeks to be the "natural" form of social organization.

The parental relationship serves the need for **reproduction**; that between master and slave for **production** of food, shelter and other necessary goods.

The Purpose of the City State

So, although the origin of "political economy" is the household unit, this alone is not enough to meet all needs. The co-operative effort of large numbers of people is required to build irrigation systems, defences against enemies and so on. The village is a further natural development. A final development to meet greater needs is the *polis* itself, the city-state. The principle at work here is *autarky* (*autos*, "self" and *arkeo*, "suffice") or self-sufficiency.

HUMAN SOCIAL DEVELOPMENT WILL HAVE MET ITS PURPOSE WHEN IT HAS REACHED A STAGE OF INDEPENDENCE SUCH THAT IT NEEDS NO FURTHER HELP FROM OUTSIDE.

Here again we see Aristotle, the teleological biologist. Human societies have a purpose, which is to meet the needs of people who, as individuals, lack self-sufficiency. When these needs, all of them, are met, then the society is at its most fully developed state and should remain thus.

For Aristotle, the exercise of practical wisdom in everyday life is essential for *eudaimonia*, and it is the job of the state to allow people to do so. In the end, the best kind of life for humans is one that includes practical wisdom, and that practical wisdom should be used to work towards the common good.

The Economy of Slavery

Democracy of a kind did function in some Greek city states, particularly in the Athenian sphere, and has been cherished as a political ideal of European civilization ever since. But how can democracy and slavery co-exist? That seems to us an unacceptable contradiction. The founders of the American republic, **Washington**, **Jefferson** and other patrician landowners with slaves, did not find it entirely incompatible.

AN ECONOMY OF "FREE LABOUR", WORK IN EXCHANGE FOR WAGES, IS A PHENOMENON OF 19TH CENTURY CAPITALISM.

SLAVERY, SERFDOM AND VARIOUS STAGES OF "SEMI-FREE" LABOUR HAD TO BE UNDERGONE BEFORE WE CAME TO THIS LESS THAN IDEAL CAPITALIST FORM.

KARL MARX

Slavery was fundamental to all ancient civilizations, Babylonian, Egyptian and so on, that precede the Greek and Roman, and went on long after them.

Heavy production, in mining for instance, was brutal and deadly for the slave worker. But slavery was more complicated than we might think.

A MASTER OFTEN "RENTED OUT" HIS SKILLED SLAVES AS WAGE-EARNERS.

A PORTION OF THE WAGE COULD BE SAVED TO "BUY OUT" OF SLAVERY ...

*A PRACTICE KNOWN AS **MANUMISSION** THAT BECAME VERY COMMON IN ROMAN TIMES.*

Slavery is not only morally wrong but, as **Karl Marx** and other economists recognized, fatally inefficient. It brought those civilizations that relied on it to ruin and collapse. Aristotle's justification of slavery is no better than others familiar to the ancients. He argues that the slave needs the master for the "practical wisdom" that he lacks. The interesting point is that Aristotle accepts the need to defend slavery – which suggests that if it were indisputably "natural", no defence would be needed. Ideas that serve to justify unjustifiable power are called **ideology** or **false consciousness**.

What is the Best Constitution?

What kind of *polis* will best meet the needs of its citizens? What is the best kind of constitution? In typical pragmatic, empirical fashion, Aristotle tries to answer these questions by examining the constitutions of many city states. His conclusions are not democratic.

He, like Plato, had a horror of the mob, and was contemptuous of politicians who "pandered" to the mass of the people.

We must keep in mind that Aristotle's (or Plato's or any Greek thinker's) search for the best city-state constitution was not a mere abstract inquiry but a problem of real urgency. The various city states of the Mediterranean were highly competitive, often at war, and the question of "best" might be solved by which one prevailed over all others. Every type of political difference could be found in practice among these states. Many of the political terms we now use have their origins in these practices.

Tyranny: from *tyrannos*, absolute sovereign unlimited by law.

Monarchy: from *monos* (alone) *arkho* (to rule).

Anarchy: from *an* (not, without) *arkhia* (rule).

Aristocracy: from *aristos* (best) *kratia* (power, rule of).

Democracy: from *demos* (the common people) *kratia*.

Oligarchy: from *oligoi* (the few) *arkho* (to rule).

Plutocracy: from *ploutos* (wealth, riches) *kratia* ...

In the end, it was Alexander's empire that prevailed over the Greek states on a *cosmopolitan* (*cosmos*, "world" and *polites*, "citizenships") scale, until it too fell prey to another empire of the originally city-state Rome.

Rule by One or Few ...

A monarchy would be an ideal solution – but only if the king was benevolent and had almost supernatural powers of good judgement. Aristotle knows that in this world such kings are rare or unknown.

MONARCHS WILL ALMOST CERTAINLY RULE TO PROMOTE THEIR OWN ADVANTAGE.

AN ARISTOCRACY MIGHT WORK BUT, AGAIN, THE SMALL NUMBER OF RULERS PROBABLY COULD NOT BE TRUSTED ...

THEY WOULD TURN INTO AN OLIGARCHY, MAKING DECISIONS TO SERVE THEIR OWN ENDS RATHER THAN THOSE OF THE COMMUNITY AS A WHOLE.

Rule by a Middle Class

Aristotle concludes that the best practical form of government is a constitutional republic in which power is shared between the people and some kind of élite. The precise arrangements do not matter and will vary from one *polis* to another.

BUT ESSENTIAL TO THE WELL-BEING OF THE COMMUNITY IS A STRONG AND SECURE MIDDLE CLASS TO GIVE WEIGHT AND PERMANENCE TO THE POLITICAL PROCESS.

What does Aristotle mean by a "middle class"? Certainly not a middle class in modern capitalist terms. It is a class of middle-sized landowners, usually slave-owners, who enjoy financial leisure to think constructively. He does not include artisans and merchants who were often *metics*, that is, like himself, migrant foreigners from other city states without full citizen status. He has in mind, as usual, a "mean", a class midway between excess wealth and economic dependence.

The Politics of Education

Aristotle's *Politics* concludes with an unfinished sketch of education. The importance of education in creating good citizens of a *polis* was already a concern of pre-Socratic thinkers and what Aristotle has to say does not seem new. He emphasizes once again, as in his *Ethics*, the value of "good habits". The point of good laws is to "make good citizens by accustoming them to be good". Aristotle's aim is to produce the **citizen-ruler**. What does he mean?

*I MEAN, SOMEONE WHO IS CAPABLE OF **ARCHEIN** AND **ARCHESTHAI** - TO RULE AND BE RULED.*

*THIS IS SIMILAR TO WHAT I SAID IN MY **LAWS**.*

Aristotle endorses Plato's views on the state regulation of marriage, rearing of infants and discipline of children. But there is also a crucial difference between them.

Aristotle's ideal is the all-round good man – able, virtuous, dignified and courteous, magnanimous and liberal, as well as courageous, just and self-disciplined. He believed it possible to produce this "good citizen" by training and practice. Plato instead did not believe education was enough. He devised a system of checks, controls and censorship enforced by a council of vigilantes to police the behaviour of citizens.

That is the difference: Aristotle is planning an Ideal State that can produce the **right kind of life** he would like; Plato devises one for other "ordinary" people, not himself.

Politics, Education and Art

Aristotle's thoughts on the politics of education lead him to consider the value of music, art and literature in the formation of the citizen-ruler. Here again he will differ radically from Plato. Aristotle's view is that the **non-utility** of the arts makes them suitable for the ruling class of citizens who are free of professional activities.

TO BE LOOKING ALWAYS FOR UTILITY IN EVERYTHING IS UNFITTING IN THOSE WHO ARE FREE AND WHOSE MINDS HAVE BEEN BROUGHT TO THE HIGHEST PITCH.

Studying the arts is good for the character and also a relaxation for such minds. But this leaves him with a problem – precisely the one Plato confronted and resolved in a way unacceptable to Aristotle's more liberal views.

What is the problem of art that vexed Plato, Aristotle and others? It might seem strange to us today. To be good at anything – playing the flute, painting or writing – requires constant practice of that skill.

IT BECOMES A **PROFESSION**, A **TRADE**, NO DIFFERENT IN THIS SENSE THAN MAKING A GOOD PAIR OF SHOES.

THAT'S THE PROBLEM. YOU BECOME THE SLAVE OF A TRADE AND THEREFORE UNFREE ...

Skilled professionals of all kinds were not properly "citizens" but an underclass of *banausoi*, artisans or trades-people. The historian **Plutarch** (*c.* AD 46-120) spoke for an élite when he said: "We admire the art but despise the artist." So, how can a free citizen benefit from art without being tainted by professionalism? Before we come to Aristotle's reply, let us examine Plato's condemnation of art.

Plato's Condemnation of Art

It has been said that Plato valued art so highly, he ended up banishing it from his ideal republic. Plato has two arguments for ridding his state of the arts.

FIRST, ART IS A DANGEROUS ILLUSION. IT IS A COPY OF A WORLD WHICH IS ITSELF AN INFERIOR COPY OF THE REAL WORLD OF IDEAL FORMS.

SECOND, NOT ONLY IS ART THE "IMITATION OF AN IMITATION", BUT ALSO IT ENCOURAGES IN YOUNG PEOPLE THE BAD HABIT OF ARTISTIC IMITATION WHICH BELONGS TO ARTISANS.

Not only do poets and artists "tell lies", not only is art a *banausic* bad habit, but, worse yet, it ignites desires and passions that prevent us from being the calm intellectual observers required of well-behaved citizens.

Aristotle's Poetics

What is Aristotle's answer to that? His reply in the *Poetics* is surprisingly modern. He is the first to ask the question "What is art?", and to do so with scientific impartiality that lays the foundations of Western aesthetics still valid today. There are several words in Greek essential to our understanding of his theory of art …

1. TECHNE: craft

> IT IS OFTEN SAID THAT THE GREEKS HAD NO WORD FOR "ART", ONLY *TECHNE*, WHICH REFERS TO ANY *TECHNICAL SKILL* - SHOE-MAKING AND CARPENTRY, AS WELL AS MUSIC, PAINTING OR POETRY.

> BUT OUR OWN WORD "ART" ISN'T MUCH BETTER. WE HAVE TO ADD "FINE" TO DISTINGUISH SCULPTURE AND PAINTING FROM THE ART OF COOKERY OR MOTORCYCLE MAINTENANCE.

Techne is not only a "craft" but also an ingenuity, a means or set of rules by which a thing is gained, very like the old Saxon root of "wise", meaning "wit".

Techne and Mimesis

Aristotle's view of *techne* is that of ingenuity, a question of the artist's **thought**, which is deliberate, rational and constructs its object by observable rules. For the first time in history, art is permitted an **autonomy** never considered before: it is an activity with its own logic.

2. MIMESIS: imitation

> *I ACCEPT THAT ART IS AN **IMITATION** – BUT NOT SIMPLY A COPY OR AN ILLUSION.*

Imitation depends on thinking and on the resources of language or other physical means to *re*-produce experience. Art is therefore a **representation** of our reflection on the sensuous appearance of things.

3. POIESIS: "to give form", hence "poetry", conveys well the sense of what art does. Artists give representational form to a piece of matter that is totally unlike the original. Those famous shoes by **Vincent Van Gogh** (1853-90) are made of paint and canvas, not a "real" copy of them from "real" leather. Aristotle attributes a particularity to aesthetic artefacts that must not be confused, as Plato does, with merely "copying" something that **already has** a form.

NOT TO KNOW THAT A HIND HAS NO HORNS IS A LESS SERIOUS MATTER THAN TO PAINT IT INARTISTICALLY.

It is a question for Aristotle of appreciating the artistry, not the accuracy of the imitation. But what do words represent in terms of *mimesis*? Poetry, he says, imitates "men in action" and states of mind.

Higher Than History

Poetry is Aristotle's generic term for the fictions of drama, epic and other genres. He states: "… it is not the function of the poet to relate what has happened, but **what may happen** – what is possible according to the law of probability or necessity". He compares history with poetry and arrives at a surprising, even shocking, verdict.

*POETRY IS A MORE PHILOSOPHICAL AND HIGHER THING THAN HISTORY: FOR POETRY TENDS TO EXPRESS THE **UNIVERSAL**, HISTORY THE **PARTICULAR**.*

To write convincingly of what might "probably happen" means that the poet understands the universal laws of what by necessity **could** happen. And that is superior to any report of what has already happened. Aristotle endows fiction with an almost prophetic power.

Tragedy and Katharsis

Aristotle seems the first not only to define what art properly **is** but also what it **does**. For him, the proper function (*ergon*, literally "the work") of tragic drama is to arouse "pity and fear" and at the same time to effect the *katharsis* or purgation of these emotions.

4. KATHARSIS (usually written *catharsis*): *purgation*

> *ARISTOTLE REMEMBERS HIS MEDICAL TRAINING ...*

> *TRAGEDY IS A FORM OF **HOMEOPATHIC TREATMENT** - CURING EMOTION BY MEANS OF AN EMOTION LIKE IN KIND BUT NOT IDENTICAL.*

This is his answer – his "pharmaceutical remedy" – to Plato's fear that poetry damages us by arousing unnecessary passions and should be prohibited. It also answers: "What is the use of art?" Citizens benefit from art by acquiring detached, free and critical judgement of what it **represents**.

Aristotle's Unities

Aristotle's description of tragedy suggests that its events should be unified by one story. This became known as the "unity of action". An Italian theorist, **Lodovico Castelvetro** (1505-71) elaborated this principle into a system of "Aristotelian Rules" that demands unity of action, place and time.

*A PLAY SHOULD HAVE **ONE PLOT**, OCCUR IN **ONE PLACE** AND IN THE SPACE OF **ONE DAY**.*

DOES A DAY MEAN 12 OR 24 HOURS?

DOES A SINGLE PLACE MEAN A ROOM, A HOUSE OR A TOWN?

CASTELVETRO

CORNEILLE

RACINE

Despite such confusions, these rigid rules were adopted in France by the classical tragedians **Pierre Corneille** (1606-84) and **Jean Racine** (1639-99) to produce works of great power.

Aristotle did not prescribe any such rules. His aim was descriptive, not prescriptive. Moreover, his experience of tragedy was limited to dramas in which "pity and fear" are inspired by the misfortune of personages superior to ourselves, great kings like Agamemnon or Oedipus, or princely figures like Orestes.

THEIR DOWNFALL IS BROUGHT ABOUT NOT BY VICE BUT BY SOME GREAT ERROR OR FRAILTY OF CHARACTER ...

*WHAT ABOUT OTHELLO'S **JEALOUSY**, OR MACBETH'S **AMBITION**? ARE THESE VICES, ERRORS OR FLAWS?*

Shakespeare did not abide by the pattern of "classical rules". Nor does a modern tragedy like Arthur Miller's *Death of a Salesman* (1947), in which the protagonist Willie Loman's flaw is an innocent belief in the American Dream.

The Uses of Rhetoric

Rhetoric is now taken simply as insincere or windy speech. But for Aristotle and other Greek thinkers, it was a crucial *techne* – the skill or art of **persuasion** in political, legal and other forms of disputation. Skill in speaking was of vital importance.

Aristotle characteristically took a more tolerant and systematic view of rhetoric. For him, it was a branch of logic and a counterpart to dialectics.

Dialectics dealt with matters necessarily and always true; rhetoric with matters that are probable – a "logic of probability" related to poetics. Rhetoric is a valid method to solve problems and reach conclusions in law and politics, in areas where things are "for the most part true".

Marshall McLuhan (1911-80), in his studies of advertising and the mass media, foreshadowed the tactics of postmodernist "deconstruction", for instance, of Julia Kristeva (b.1941) and Jacques Derrida (b.1930) who rely on the semiotics outlined by Aristotle.

The Legacy of Aristotle

Aristotelian ideas continued to be taught in Athens in one form or another until AD 529, when the Roman Emperor Justinian in Christian Byzantium closed all the philosophical schools. Shortly after Aristotle's death, the Lyceum attracted as many as 2,000 students and was very influential. During the third century BC, other important philosophical schools added to and developed the Aristotelian perspective, such as the Epicureans, the Stoics and the Sceptics.

FOLLOWING THE ENFORCED CLOSURES, WE FLED ACROSS THE AEGEAN SEA ...

AND CONTINUED TEACHING ARISTOTLE'S DOCTRINES IN PERSIA, ARMENIA AND SYRIA.

HIS IDEAS AND WRITINGS WERE ABSORBED INTO ARABIC THINKING IN ABOUT THE MIDDLE OF THE 9TH CENTURY.

Study of his work also continued in the eastern Roman empire at Byzantium.

Aristotle and Islamic Science

Causality, the structure of intellectual knowledge and logic were three features that impressed Arab philosophers. Logic used on Greek problems could also be applied to new ones inspired by Islamic tradition. The rationalist ideal of *falsafah* (Arabized form of "philosophy") incorporated the aim of living rationally according to the governing laws of the universe.

Before Europe

The *fayllasufs* (philosophers) came to know truth through logic and insight. Ordinary people can reach truth only through symbols. Therefore, science could flourish – it was the rational exploration of the world made by God. In early medieval Western Europe, such activity could not take place, because it would tend to contradict scriptures. But in the Arabic east, at that time, no such conflict existed.

During the first millennium, Aristotle's work was more or less unknown in Western Europe. All this changed in the 12th century when Arabic scholars took his work to Moorish Spain.

The commentaries on Aristotle by the Arabic scholars **Avicenna** (980-1037) and **Averroes** (c. 1126-98) were particularly influential. Once translated into Latin, Aristotle's works were studied extensively.

By a curious twist of fate, European advances in science would come from Arabic Aristotelianism and yet, as we will see, it was precisely this "spirit of science" in 17th-century Europe that turned against Aristotle.

Albert the Great and Thomas Aquinas

The relationship between Aristotelian thought and Christianity was ambiguous but crucial. He was, of course, a pagan, and so initially the Church was hostile to his philosophy. Indeed, in AD 1210, anyone who studied his natural philosophy was threatened with excommunication. Nevertheless, study of his work continued, especially after the Crusaders discovered manuscripts of his work in Greek in Constantinople, which could be translated straight into Latin. The Dominican priest **Albert the Great** (c. 1200-80) used Aristotle's methods and work to explain the natural world as he found it.

I BEGAN WHAT MY PUPIL AQUINAS CONTINUED ...

... TO INTEGRATE ARISTOTLE'S TRUTHS WITH THOSE OF CHRISTIAN THEOLOGY, AND THEREBY GIVE IT A LOGICAL, PHILOSOPHICAL BASIS.

In this he was successful, despite the doubts of many in the Church, and Aristotle remained the dominant figure in philosophy, science and all

intellectual life for several centuries.

The Decline of Aristotelianism

This dominance was a bad thing. Speculation and scientific research that seemed to go beyond Aristotle were discouraged and many now associate the philosophy of the period, usually known as *scholasticism*, with dogmatism and resistance to new ideas. **Cesare Cremonini** (1550-1631), a Paduan Aristotelian scholar, refused to look through Galileo's (**Galileo Galilei** 1564-1642) telescope.

IN CASE IT MIGHT CHALLENGE ARISTOTLE'S INTERPRETATION OF THE UNIVERSE.

BUT, IN THE FACE OF OBVIOUS CONTRADICTIONS, ARISTOTELIAN THOUGHT LOST CREDIBILITY.

During the 17th century, its intellectual foundations were demolished by **Francis Bacon** (1561-1626) and **Robert Boyle** (1627-91), the founders of a new empiricist method. **Thomas Hobbes** (1588-1679) said: "Scarce anything can be more absurdly said in natural philosophy, than that which is now called Aristotle's *Metaphysics*." The dogmatism of the Aristotelian Schoolmen came near to destroying Aristotle's work.

Is Aristotle "Scientific"?

The chief accusation made by such 17th-century empiricists was that Aristotle was **unscientific**. Ironic, if we consider his lifetime project of describing a scientifically comprehensible world. But what is meant by a "comprehensible world"? A major **paradigm shift** had occurred in viewing the world. Aristotle was a pagan who asked pagan questions.

WHAT ARE THE SUBSTANCES THAT THE WORLD CONTAINS? WHAT ARE HUMANS AS A SPECIAL KIND OF SUBSTANCE?

CHRISTIANITY ELEVATES HUMANS INTO MORE THAN A "SPECIAL KIND OF SUBSTANCE".

THEY ARE UNIQUE IN THE WORLD, WITH A SOUL AND AN ETERNAL DESTINY DENIED TO EVERYTHING ELSE.

Descartes' Doubt

By the 17th century, this Christian "specialness" of the human being
had turned into a radical self-consciousness that perceives the world in
both empirical and sceptical terms. **René Descartes** (1596-1650), a
mathematician with interests in geometry, optics and physics, introduced
a **subjective element** into epistemology: "How do we know **for certain**
that we know?"

This plunged philosophy into a sceptical quagmire from which it has not
yet emerged. Aristotle's plain account of the world, without any profound
account of how we **apprehend** it, came to seem pedestrian and naïve.

Does Empiricism Eliminate Doubt?

Descartes' doubt might seem neatly resolved by Bacon's empiricism. Bacon emphasized the primacy of induction and experimentation, rather than Aristotle's unrigorous observation.

*EXPERIMENTS HAVE TO BE **REPRODUCIBLE** TO ESTABLISH WHICH FACTORS ARE ALWAYS **PRESENT** - OR ALWAYS **ABSENT** - IN THE PHENOMENA WE STUDY.*

*BACON ANTICIPATED MY PRINCIPLE THAT **FALSIFICATION** IS AS IMPORTANT AS CONFIRMATION IN SCIENTIFIC PROCEDURE.*

KARL POPPER (1902-94), PHILOSOPHER OF SCIENCE.

Bacon gave greater significance to Aristotle's efficient cause and downgraded the other kinds. But his methodology did not dispose of Descartes' problem of subjective uncertainty – on the contrary, as we will next see.

Hume's Scepticism

The Scottish Enlightenment philosopher **David Hume** (1711-76) pursued these questions of self-knowledge, belief and causation. A scientific study of human nature reveals that the mind obeys the laws of association, which means that our key beliefs – for instance, **cause** – are products of the imagination, not reasoning.

*WE ARE HABITUATED TO EXPECT A NATURAL SEQUENCE OF "CAUSE AND EFFECT", WHICH ASCRIBES TO NATURE A NECESSITY THAT IS ONLY **PSYCHOLOGICAL**.*

CAUSE

*HUME'S VIEW IS THAT OUR CONCEPTS ARE SIMPLY **INDUCED** BELIEFS ...*

THAT CAN'T BE RIGHT.

EFFECT

Immanuel Kant (1724-1804) set out, in his *Critique of Pure Reason* (1781-87), to secure the foundations of human cognition.

Kant's Theory of Knowledge

Kant agrees with Hume that knowledge rests on experience. But he rejects the notion that concepts, such as cause, are only psychological. Kant returns to Aristotle's ideas of the *categories* and the distinction between *a priori* and *a posteriori* knowledge. *A priori* knowledge is prior to and does not depend on experience; *a posteriori* comes after and does rely on it. Kant argues that it is impossible to know anything *a priori* about the world **as it is**, independently of our **cognitive apparatus**. He turns Hume's argument upside-down ...

*... BECAUSE WE POSSESS **A PRIORI** CONCEPTS, WHICH ENABLE US TO EXPERIENCE THE WORLD, WE CAN THEN MAKE **A POSTERIORI** CLAIMS ABOUT THE WAY IT APPEARS TO US ...*

*FOR INSTANCE, **SPACE** AND **TIME** ARE **A PRIORI**, OR PRE-CONDITIONS, OF OUR KNOWLEDGE.*

*AND YOU BORROWED MY "CATEGORIES" TO IDENTIFY THESE **A PRIORI** CONCEPTS WHICH ARE NECESSARY TO HUMAN UNDERSTANDING.*

The Importance of Aristotle Today

Kant's theory is a limited return to Aristotle but does not entirely eliminate scepticism. Yet it does allow us to reaffirm the potency of Aristotle's metaphysics. If our knowledge of the world has meaning then, surely, we must be in some direct and unambiguous mental contact with that world. On this assumption, Aristotle described a theory of **what underlies** the evident world with great confidence.

Other aspects of Aristotle's thought remain important today.

▶ Especially, his work on moral psychology and virtue ethics, at the forefront of philosophical thinking, inspires the contemporary political and social doctrine of communitarianism at the basis of centre and centre-left modern politics.

▶ Aristotle's virtue theory forms a "third way" between a hard-edged materialist reduction of human action to genetic and bio-chemical causation on the one hand, and on the other an unsustainable dualism involving non-material entities such as "souls" or "rights" that people have simply by being human.

▶ We have also seen how Aristotle's ideas on **aesthetics** and **semiotics** continue to be relevant and challenging to the postmodern impasse in the cultural areas.

We might end by saying that in general Aristotle's **realism** is a benevolent influence on politics, ethics, art, philosophy and science.

Further Reading

As I have said elsewhere, reading Aristotle in the original is not an easy experience. The works were probably not intended for public consumption, and some guidance is helpful. People have been writing about Aristotle's writings for thousands of years now, and there is plenty to choose from, much of it discussing what he actually meant rather than what he said. On the other hand, reading the Master in the original reveals a depth and texture which is ultimately profoundly rewarding.

Aristotle in Outline by Timothy A. Robinson (Hackett Publishing, 1995) is a useful overview for non-specialists, as is **Aristotle** from the "Great Philosophers" series by Kenneth McLeish (Routledge, 1999). Also worth looking at are David Ross's classic account, **Aristotle** (Routledge, 1995), and **Aristotle the Philosopher** by J.L. Ackrill (Oxford Paperbacks, 1981). I found **The Cambridge Companion to Aristotle**, edited by Jonathan Barnes (Cambridge University Press, 1995), particularly useful. Look also at **Introduction to Aristotle**, edited by Richard McKeon (Modern Library, 1992).

The general reader will also be helped in their understanding of Aristotle if they have some idea of the context within which he was working. There is much available on Ancient Greek philosophy, but a good place to begin might be **Before and After Socrates** by Francis Cornford (Cambridge University Press, 1932). Plato's work is particularly important in understanding Aristotle, and for help with this I can recommend no better book for the beginner than Dave Robinson's **Introducing Plato**, in this series (Icon Books, 2000). Martha Nussbaum and Richard Sorabji are both powerful and important writers who have much to say about the relevance of ancient Greek concerns for today. For example, Nussbaum's **The Fragility of Goodness** (Cambridge University Press, 2001) is one I look forward to reading when it is published next year. A more challenging book is G.E.R. Lloyd's **Aristotelian Explorations** (Cambridge University Press, 1999)

Those interested in Aristotle's impact on the middle ages may like to look at **Aristotle and Aristotelianism in Medieval Muslim, Jewish and Christian Philosophy** by Hussain Kassim (Austin and Winfield, 1996). There are many books on particular aspects of his work, such as the politics, the metaphysics and so on. Some are rather daunting, such as W.D. Ross's **Aristotle: Metaphysics** (Oxford University Press, 1924), which runs to over a thousand pages. However, I have always found James Urmson's **Aristotle's Ethics** valuable and approachable. Readers may also like to take a look at **Aristotle on the Perfect Life** by Anthony Kenny (Clarendon Press, 1996) or **Feminist Interpretations of Aristotle**, edited by Cynthia Freeland (Pennsylvania State University Press, 1998).

Acknowledgements

The author of **Introducing Aristotle** would like to thank his wife for her patience while he wrote this book, his editor Richard Appignanesi and, in particular, Dave Robinson, who has been the best colleague a teacher could expect, and without whom the book would not have been written at all.

Judy Groves thanks Howard Peters, Madeline Fenton, Oscar Zarate and Arabella Anderson for their generous help.

Index